FLY FISHING

FLY FISHING

A LIFE IN MID-STREAM

Recollections and Essays

TURHAN TIRANA

Kensington Books

KENSINGTON BOOKS are published by

Kensington Publishing Corp.
850 Third Avenue
New York, NY 10022

Copyright © 1996 by Turhan Tirana

Publisher and author acknowledge with gratitude permission to use the following copyrighted material:

The Complete Fly Fisherman: The Notes and Letters of Theodore Gordon, edited by John McDonald, used by permission of Lyons & Burford, Publishers.

American Fly Fishing, by Paul Schullery, © 1987 by Paul Schullery, used by permission of Lyons & Burford, Publishers.

Fly Fishing Through the Midlife Crisis, © 1993 by Howell Raines, used by permission of William Morrow and Company, Inc., New York.

Last Call of the Wild, by Jonathan Raban, published in the April 1995 issue of *Esquire,* used by permission of *Esquire.*

Art Flick's New Streamside Guide, by Art Flick, used by permission of Crown Publishers, Inc.

Library of Congress Card Catalog Number: 96-075280

ISBN 1-57566-031-8

First Printing: May, 1996

10 9 8 7 6 5 4 3 2 1

Printed in the United States of America

ACKNOWLEDGMENTS

In addition to those who consented to be quoted and whose names appear in the text that follows, I first would like to thank three women: my agent, sometime fishing partner, and wife, Denise Marcil, who made this book possible and provided advice and encouragement throughout its writing; my publisher, Lynn Brown, whose idea the book was; and my editor, Sarah Gallick, who helped me stay focused. Thanks go to Terry Brykczyski for his help with the illustrations. I'd also like to thank Scott Matthews, occasional fishing buddy and font of ideas; Don Walton, who before me described *Ephemerella dorothea,* a mayfly, as a person; and my mother, Rosamond Tirana, who supported and provisioned my early angling ventures and whose keen eye for the superfluous shaped the book.

CONTENTS

PREFACE

This book is written for those who aspire to experience the enchantment of fly-fishing, those who are just curious about the sport, and those who already fly-fish and might find in my musings confirmation of their own thoughts and feelings, and thereby some satisfaction.

The format is the essay, with an emphasis on personal experience. I make no attempt at instruction on techniques, hints or tips on becoming a better angler, or recommendations of places to fish. Others are more skilled at fly-fishing than I, more knowledgeable about ichthyology, aquatic entomology, and environmental conservation, better traveled and catch more fish.

What I bring to the reader is a desire to share my love of the sport, and to relate some experiences that illustrate its merits. My experience as an angler spans fifty years, and in a sense, this book has been in gestation since I was nine years old. A lot has been written about fly-fishing over the past five hundred years, and some of it is very good. I see this book supplementing that writing tradition with a perspective born of our time and place.

Fly-fishing is different from just fishing. It's at the high end of the sport in terms of skills, and it requires collecting a good deal of information that most people would consider esoteric, which is to say, useless in any other endeavor. It also requires curiosity and maybe even a bit of aggression. Fly-fishing is not relaxing in the common sense of the word. It's unlike, say, daydreaming in the shade of a tree beside a bucolic lake while holding a rod at the end of which dangles a line and gently squirming worm. Fly-fishing is active; something is happening every moment, and the fly-fisher to be successful must stay alert. People who like fly-fishing tend to be demanding and impatient, although their quest is ultimately, in my view, peace of the spirit.

Fly-fishing today is in vogue in some circles. A lot of people like the image fly-fishing evokes and the associations that accompany it, including, probably, the sense that this is something special for special people. Some fly-fishermen, including me, think what we're in the midst of a fad that in due course will fade away. The sport has been romanticized of late in books and one major movie, hyped up by a large and growing population who make a living off it. Fly-fishing also has been made easier by technological advances, including lighter and more finely balanced rods and lines that allow a person to cast reasonably well in a short time, and a lot of new data on fish habits and habitats. The truth is that fly-fishing is still difficult; it takes time to master and requires coping with more than the norm of frustrations. Good casting is only the beginning; one also must know what flies to use, and where and how to present them to fish that one must believe are there even if they aren't. Pretty soon, those who come to the sport with a mental picture of themselves in designer fly-fishing clothing, casting flawlessly over pristine waters accessible only to the privileged and connected to the eternal by some grace limited to the bright and successful, will become fed up with the demands of reality. They'll find easier ways to convey the appearance of what they want to be without so much trouble.

For those who survive the rites of passage, the rewards are worth the effort. For those so disposed there are rewards for the soul as well as the mind. One theme worked hard by many writers on fishing, especially Juliana Berners, a fifteenth-century prioress, and Izaak Walton, who followed her a century and a half later, is that mucking about nature can at least improve one's sense of well-being, and perhaps also bring one closer to the core of life.

There is a magic in fly-fishing born of faith and immersion in nature that's expressed in the tenth-century Zen poet Setcho:

> Spring light, soft bank mist,
> And on the still water his boat.
> He grips in his dream a thousand-foot line,
> Match for the greatest whale.

This book attempts to describe that magic.

FLY FISHING

1

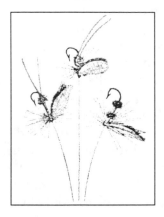

FIRST FISH

T he fascination with fishing must be innate. No one in my family had fished for sport or livelihood. In fact, at the age of nine, I don't recall even knowing anyone who had fished. Nonetheless, I was drawn to fishing as if by the hand of God, or at least some larger power outside myself. There was nothing I could do to resist the call even had I wanted to, which I didn't. My answering it seemed as natural as breathing, and as necessary.

The setting of my first fishing venture was the island of Nantucket in Massachusetts, known better as the world's principal whaling port in the early nineteenth century. My family vacationed there.

In the realm of sports fishing, Nantucket, thirty miles at sea, is known as a premier location for large, predatory bluefish and striped bass. It is not known at all for freshwater fishing.

However, with no background in sports fishing and no one to turn to for advice, saltwater fishing for me at that time was out of the question. Nonetheless, not far from our house, over a moor with clumps of stunted pines, was a pond where I imagined there might lurk smaller, gentler versions of blues and bass.

The first time I saw the pond was at a cocktail party given by the owners of the property that included the pond. One of their purposes was to introduce my brother Bardyl and me to their two daughters, who were our age. The daughter my age, Diana, was pretty and poised. I was not disappointed, and in a few years it would be she who would fascinate me. However, at that time, my eyes were drawn more to the pond. Although no more than an acre in size, the pond seemed to my nine-year-old eyes just a smaller version of the ocean. It was separated from the ocean by a sand dune covered with spartina grass. Surrounding the pond was a near-impenetrable wall of bushes, cattails, and other forbidding vegetation. The water, in the sunlight, was a blue so dark as to convey the possibility that the pond could be bottomless. It was a font of mystery, containing who-knows-what creatures. Perhaps whatever was there would explain the reason for life and my place in its scheme.

Nothing could possibly have been more important in my life than access to that pond. The problem of a four-foot-high barrier of thickly tangled underbrush was solvable, I saw, by a small rowboat, white paint peeling from wood slats, which was slightly but ominously submerged in the water. No oars were in sight.

Following the party, the sisters and we met from time to time. As it turned out, however, their agenda proved different from mine. They were interested in Bardyl and me as boys, as creatures of the other sex and an opportunity to test their developing feminine wiles. Adventure was what was on our minds. Bardyl and I became friendly enough with the girls to feel we could ask to use the boat. Their parents readily agreed, and the father pulled a pair of oars out of the garage for us.

Somewhere I had found an old rig consisting of short fiberglass rod, linen line, and what is known as a bait casing reel (now used in a much improved, sophisticated version in tournament freshwater black bass fishing). Spinning reels had not yet been invented. I also found some rusty hooks with metal fins, known as spinners, that spun around the shank when pulled through the water.

The boat was tied up to the shore. Bardyl, acting as fellow adventurer and confidant-in-life, helped me bail the water out of the boat's bottom with a rusted can. With Bardyl's wordless, wide-eyed presence providing me with approbation and encouragement, I rowed out, stood up, and cast. I incurred the then-usual difficulty with backlash, when the speed of the reel is faster than the speed of the line leaving the reel, and the line tangled inside the reel in horrible messes. Eventually, I succeeded in making a few backlash-free casts. My concentration narrowed, and my awareness of most everything else around me, including Bardyl, vanished in the anticipation of . . . I knew not what.

In due course, I felt a tug at the end of the line. Instantly, I was connected to life somewhere in the blue deepness of the pond. Time stopped. My heart pounded. Nothing existed but the creature I felt through the line, struggling to be free of me. I felt my being depended on finding what was there. A combination of primordial cunning and modern mechanics allowed me to maintain through the reel just the right tension in the line. After what seemed an eternity but in fact mustn't have been more than three or four minutes, I pulled the fish to the side of the boat. What I saw was an eleven-inch yellow perch. I was thrilled. Looking down at the fish wavering just under the surface, I felt as I thought God must feel, in command and at one with creation.

The next task was to transport the fish from water to boat bottom, from its world to mine, where I could examine it.

Later I learned I could become closer still to the fish world by handling them. However, at that time I was uncertain whether the perch could bite, whether the spines could cut, and whether the fish was scarily slimy. Taking the prudent approach, I grabbed the line and swung the fish gingerly into the boat. By luck, the hook held.

The perch was transformed from a metaphor for the mystery of life to something more immediate and even better, an object of magnificent beauty. Shiny green-black bars alternated with a lighter olive background on its sides, and bright golden, orange side and bottom fins glistened in the sun like an enormous, live jewel.

What happened next I don't recall. That was fifty years ago. Probably, Bardyl and I took the fish home to be admired by our parents and dealt with, somehow, by our mother. However, by then the once-enchanting perch would have lost its luster as well as its magic and become just a dead fish. Its ultimate fate was irrelevant. The principal event was the catching of the fish and my brief connection to the mystery that was the source of life.

That was the start.

During the next several years, my fishing compulsion incubated within me. I actually fished only a little, sometimes with Bardyl and sometimes alone but never where fishing was especially productive.

I recall even fishing in Washington, D.C., our regular home, at Pierce's Mill in Rock Creek Park, an idyllic spot with a pretty stream flowing between lawns with hardwood trees and over a stone dam that provided the power for an old grist mill that survives as a museum. I fished below the dam peacefully and full of anticipation. Normally, tail waters of dams are great fishing spots. However, Rock Creek was not normal. It was polluted. At best, the toxicity would permit the survival of a few garbage-feeding suckers. Nonetheless, the scenery and my faith were such that I was able to fool myself. I never caught a fish, even a sucker, but I did succeed in satisfying my urge to fish.

In due course, I found a smaller, not quite so idyllic stream flowing out of a private water company reservoir in suburban Virginia. A shallow, rock-studded pool at the bottom of the dam that contained the reservoir also held crappie, a rather unattractive, bony, warm-water fish. Bardyl and I together with a few friends caught countless crappie there. They weren't much challenge, and after the novelty of discovering the fish and actually catching them, fishing there lost its appeal.

Those days I also took to reading about fishing. The Dr. Spock of the sort of fishing that interested me was Ray Bergman. Bergman began fishing in the early part of the century and in due course became fishing editor for *Outdoor Life*. He wrote a book, first published in 1938, called *Trout*, which at four hundred and thirty-one pages was the longest book ever written on one kind of fish. It was also good, in a comfortable, easy way, and was so popular that for many years trout fishermen didn't see any point in reading to say nothing of buying any other.

Adding to the book's allure were seventeen color plates of some six hundred beautifully painted flies, two plates of metal and feather lures for the spinning rigs just coming on the market, and one plate of thirty-six fly-tying feathers, some from birds from faraway lands. These birds are now decreed endangered, and their feathers can no longer be legally imported. The flies in the Bergman book were lined up on the plates in an order that seemed to reflect an immutable authority. I used to stare at them, entranced. Most were designed to attract fish, not to imitate specific flies, perhaps because Bergman and the anglers he knew fished mostly for eastern brook trout, which are less finicky about what they swallow than other trout. The painted flies were gorgeous. I tried to memorize the patterns and the fanciful names that seemed more suited to race horses. Included were Thunder Smart, Parmachene Beau, Greenwell's Glory, Bottle Imp, Toodle Bug, and Yellow Sally. Few of those flies are used any longer. Like women's apparel, they come in and out of fashion. Now what prevail are more realistic imitations of aquatic insects, the colors of which are muted. I wonder whether because of the many colors that assault our eyes these days, I'd be as taken with those plates if I saw them for the first time.

I also read the monthly magazines *Outdoor Life* and *Field & Stream*. One *Outdoor Life* cover mesmerized me. The illustration was of a fly-fisherman standing in a stream, casting a long, looping line over a sun-flecked pool. However, the real magic was in the maple tree in the foreground. The sun behind it gave its new spring leaves a translucence that was glorious. The picture conveyed the essence of what I thought heaven must be, peace in the midst of beauty. Momentarily, I was transported there, and I was at peace. The picture also conveyed the notion that fly-fishing might be the highest form of fishing and, perhaps, that I should aspire to learning how to fly-fish.

I dreamed of the picture becoming real, of my being transported into the body of the painted angler and actually fly-fishing on a trout stream. However, I had no idea how this could happen. All I knew about fly-fishing came from reading. I knew no adults who fished, to say nothing of fly-fished. I didn't even know where to look for a trout stream. For the time being, the dream would have to suffice. In fact, for all I knew, the dream might be all I'd have.

2

WHO FLY-FISHES

ho fly-fishes? And why?

Originally, fly-fishers were an elite group. Until not so long ago, only the propertied classes and the clergy had the leisure to fish for pleasure, to say nothing of the inclination to study the habits of game fish and the insects they eat. Most of the world was just too busy surviving.

Times have changed; a lot more people have time in which to do what they like. Fly-fishers no longer need be of the social elite or even well-to-do. In my local chapter of Trout Unlimited, a national conservation group, the membership includes the lawyers, bankers, and doctors one might expect and also construction workers, a fireman, a plumber, commercial painters, and owners of a haberdashery, a photo lab, and a curtain sales business. Occasional difficulties arise from what are mistakenly heard as slights, but generally everyone gets along. Profession and financial worth mean nothing. What counts is our common interest in fly-fishing. For most of us, fly-fishing is just about the best thing we can think of doing. We understand that the other person feels the same way, and therefore we understand and appreciate and usually like each other.

Other than through a certain intensity of spirit and occasional arguments over the fine points of their sport, one couldn't readily identify a fly-fisher. Some are fat, some thin; some jovial, some lachrymose; some loquacious, some taciturn; some Republican, some Democrat; some are in better circumstances in life, others worse; most are men, a few are women.

In addition to recreational preference, fly-fishers share the experience of years of frustration, disappointment, and expense to learn to fling a heavy line so that a tiny imitation fly made of feathers and fur lands not in a nearby tree but gently on just the spot for the current to carry it to a waiting fish, or to where a fish could be reasonably expected to be waiting. Fly-fishers also share a body of knowledge that includes aquatic entomology, fish habitat and behavior, varieties of equipment and its use, and a myriad of other skills and information that have no importance outside fly-fishing.

In fly-fishing, virtually nothing is assured, especially whether one is going to catch fish. Thus, faith that the effort undertaken will eventually culminate in catching fish is a *sina qua non*. Many fly-fishers know that the faith that one is going to catch fish leads to faith in the possibility of another, more precious catch, namely, peace of the soul.

The symbolism is obvious. Immersion in water was used by John the Baptist and later as a manifestation of the purification of sins. The early Christians also chose fish as a symbol of divine providence, and spiritual as well as physical sustenance. In the time of the Roman persecutions, they used the outline of a fish as a code to identify each other. One would draw half a fish in the ground; if the other completed the outline, he or she could be assumed to be a believer. The first letters of the word "fish" in Greek also were configured to read the word "Christ," another code. The choice of fish as a Christian symbol may have been based as much on the prevalence of fish as food in the eastern Mediterranean area as the fish's seminally pleasing shape.

Grace, in the religious sense, plays a role in fly-fishing. Some anglers are "chosen," others not. Stated another way, in equal circumstances, some anglers catch more fish than others. In a sense, one may consider that the more successful anglers in these situations have been blessed with what can only be described as a gift that others don't have, at least to the same degree. On more than one occasion I've stood back to back or shoulder to shoulder with an angler with no more experience than I, using just the same fly, fishing the same current, but with greater success. The angler has tried to impart to me his skill so that I could share equally in the catch. It didn't work. The reverse has happened as well. The more successful angler has some advantage in instinct that translates itself into technique that remains hidden to the eye. Some call it the X factor. Whatever it is, it cannot be taught; it's a gift some would say from God.

The brilliance, subtlety, and variety of color of trout, each one unique, and the grace of their shape and quickness of movement are such that few can fail to wonder at the mystery that led to their creation. The mystery is compounded by the environment of the fish, beautiful in its own right, and alien to ours. Science tells us we evolved from that environment aeons ago, but it no longer sustains us. Therefore, it's as if in capturing the fish, for the few instants they are in our grasp, we can momentarily become one with them, partake of their environment and apparent tranquility and completeness, and in the process, understand the mystery of their lives and thereby our own. For most of us, that's as far as it goes. Our unspoken, usually unconscious, quest is met by silence. But in another time or another place on a subsequent fishing trip, we might be answered. We'd find ourselves then, we may dimly expect, in harmony with creation and at peace with ourselves.

Because of this faith, born of man's unique quest to know more than how to survive, angling is seen sometimes as an activity with religious overtones. An Assyrian tablet from 2000 B.C. not only reflects this sentiment but adds this incentive; The gods do not subtract from the allotted span of men's lives the time spent fishing. The Old Testament (Deuteronomy) indicates that fish may even have been worshiped. The reader will notice in Chapter 8, "Early Fly-fishing," the same sanctification of fishing expressed by Orientals and Europeans.

Taken to an extreme, this orientation becomes pantheism which can be related to the belief of the eighteenth-century Dutch philosopher Baruch Spinoza that God is not only the cause of the world but also is to be identified with it or, in its crudest form, that God and nature are one and God can be worshiped in nature. A more common approach that reverses this thought is typified by the following portion of the Benedicte from the Episcopal *Book of Common Prayer*, derived, in turn, from the Old Testament (Psalms):

Oye Whales, and all that move in the waters,
bless ye the Lord: praise him, and magnify him for ever.

Here the fish, and all creatures, including, presumably, anglers, express their gratitude for creation to God. The Old Testament writers here certainly would agree that God blesses His creation but God is to be worshiped, not creation.

The American Indians of the Northwest worshiped fish and depended on them for survival. The mystery of these fish was enhanced by the Indians' failure to understand their biological life cycle. The Indians' best way, apparently, to connect the drifting back to sea of the rotting, blackened bodies of salmon following spawning and their reappearance a year later in full, glistening health was to think of them as immortal spirits. The intermediate stage of bright little parr emerging from the eggs evidently escaped them. The same idea was attached, generally, to herring, smelt, and other fish they caught that migrate between ocean and river.

The belief was that salmon were supernatural beings who dwelt in human form in a great house under the sea, dancing and feasting, anthropologist Philip Drucker writes. When the time came for the "run," the salmon-people put on clothes of salmon flesh, and swam into the rivers to offer themselves to the Indians.

The Indians of the Northwest believed that if some fish bones were left on land where they couldn't drift back to sea, the salmon-people, upon resurrection in human form, would lack an arm or leg or some other part. Then the tribe might refuse to ascend the river the next season. The last thing the Indians wanted to do was to offend the salmon-people. Accordingly, they developed rituals for the handling of the fish. These became so complex, specialists we might call priests had to assume responsibility for their proper conduct.

For me, it's not difficult to think of fish as part of the spiritual world, as are we and other living creatures. By way of contrast to the beliefs of the Northwest Indians, mine has no practical application; the economy in which I live affords me other ways to gather food. Nonetheless, while I do not worship fish, I think I appreciate them as much as the Northwest Indians.

In fishing, as in society, there is a hierarchy. At the bottom, most would agree, is snagging. Snagging entails throwing out a heavy line with bare treble-weighted hooks or a series of hooks into areas along river or stream banks where salmon and other fish rest on their voyage up the current to spawn. The snagger blindly jerks in his line, hoping one hook will impale a fish. A modicum of skill is required and little expenditure on equipment, and the snagger no doubt considers his endeavor a sport as well as an amusement and a means to put some food on the table.

Next in the hierarchy comes spear fishing, somewhat similar to snagging but more difficult in that one needs to target and then reach a specific fish. There follows an array of fishing with light lines carried out into the water by the weight of bait or metal or heavy plastic lures. The vast majority of fishing is in this category. The physics of fly-fishing is just the opposite, a heavy line being used to cast a feathered lure sometimes too small to even be seen unless one brings it right up to one's face.

Consider fishing for lake trout in subarctic Canada. These trout are substantially larger than their southern cousins and dwell for the most part toward the bottoms of deep lakes. A common rig to bring them to net consists of an eight-ounce hunk of lead attached to a line from a spinning (not fly) casting rod and reel. A couple of feet below the hunk of lead is a brightly painted steel spoon six inches long with a huge, single hook. Sometimes steel line is used to sink the lure even faster. To render catching these trout virtually fail-safe, sonar devices detect the fish, showing them as blips on a television-like screen with the depths in which they lie marked on the screen. One knows one has hooked one of these behemoths only by an additional heaviness at the end of the line. Is this sport? Well, yes, but the level of skill it requires is not extensive. The principal aim of the practitioners is to catch what are known as trophy trout, that is, trout that someone in some official capacity has designated as being very large and, it's understood, worthy of being stuffed and mounted. When the fisherman catches such a trout, he can be satisfied. He has a quantifiable, sanctioned measure of his success. Lake trout can be caught on occasion in shallow water on a fly rod with what's known as a streamer. A streamer consists of long feathers tied to a hook to represent small bait fish. Even with streamers, this fishing isn't a whole lot of fun. The sensation is similar to inducing to the surface a live but lethargic tire; lake trout are not great fighters.

Fly-fishing obviously is the most difficult of sport fishing, but within fly-fishing there are hierarchies as well. Some frown upon the use of large flies weighted with lead to sink them to

where fish are more likely to lie. Fishing dry flies on the surface used to be considered the epitome of fly-fishing. Dry flies
represent aquatic insects in the life stage at which they are on
the water surface drying their newly formed wings preparatory
to flying off to mate. The English angling purists of a couple
of generations ago argued whether one should cast a dry fly
only to a rising fish, not just randomly. Random casts increase
the element of luck in catching fish. Skill for the purists, not
luck, is what is valued. These days, the use of tiny emergers, a
pre–dry fly stage, that float in the surface film are coming into
prominence among the nouveaux purists. Generally, the
smaller the fly, the more credit one receives for being a sportsman.

The ultimate in angling sportsmanship may be represented
by the example of Chiang Tzu-Ya, who fished with bait but no
hook. Fly-fishers could aspire to Chiang Tzu-Ya's feeling about
angling, that the catching of fish is a superfluous aim. In any
event, the idea that catching fish to lock away in the freezer
is unnecessary is gaining credence. It is demonstrated in the
increasingly accepted practice among public fisheries policy
makers that the propagation of wild trout (trout bred where
they live) with little or no killing of fish is preferable to annual
stockings of vulnerable, easily fooled hatchery trout.

This theme is the heart of Howell Raines's *Fishing Through
a Midlife Crisis*. Raines portrays his development from what he
calls the Redneck Way in his boyhood Alabama, which is to
capture and keep as many fish as possible, in the most expe-
dient way possible, to the way of his fly-fishing mentor, which
is that the art of angling is more important than the catching.
"To achieve mastery is to rise above the need to catch fish,"
he writes. The Redneck Way brings only anxiety. Time, Raines
says, quoting a British poet, "is a rider that breaks us all, especially if our only pleasure—in football, fishing or love—
comes from keeping score."

In part because of the success of Robert Redford's movie
A River Runs Through It in conveying the beauty of fly-fishing
and some of the mystery that surrounds it, some people are

shortcutting the simple spin-fishing stage and even bypassing the Redneck Way. These new fly-fishers are not really interested in fly-fishing but in associating themselves with images that fly-fishing conveys.

Calling *A River Runs Through It* "a feature-length Ralph Lauren window display," Jonathan Raban wrote in *Esquire,* "In a rinsed sepia light, men in period leisure wear did pretty things with varnished antique fly rods. The wristy craft of casting put them in touch with the historic past, and it made them at home in nature—at home in their own natures. The grace of the line unrolling from the rod tip, the fly kissing the surface of the water as a trout rose to meet it, was pure fashion plate. Then, with the rod bent into a hoop, one could feel in the musculature of one's own forearm the burrowing shudder of the fish at the other end. In an as-yet-unspoiled Eden, we were joined to wild nature by a thread of oiled silk."

The wild, Mr. Raban continued, is growing scarce, has shot up in value, and is becoming an emblem of social status. But what does one do in the wild, he asks. Hiking is too tame and objectless for people "bred to displays of competitive prowess." Rock climbing is dangerous. Hunting "lands one in moral difficulties in mixed company." The solution is fly-fishing, at least as portrayed by the movie in "the form of an equipage of covetable goods and garments, . . . a show-off skill, and the promise of a direct line to the wild."

Fly-fishers committed to the sport for its own sake are at the other end of the scale. They are unequivocally and wholly absorbed in the sport's essentials. The Redford Way has no significance to them; they are not motivated by appearances or even by what others see as the spiritual and social rewards of fly-fishing. They do as experience and their own spirit urge.

The most essential of the essentials of fly-fishing is flies, and the creation *de nouveau* of artificial flies is at its apex. Designing a fly that works is its own reward.

One such amateur fly designer is Rick Miller, a Stamford, Connecticut, fireman and occasional guide. Rick's aim was to satisfy his own curiosity and create a dry fly with which to catch trout on a local stream in the dead of winter. The right imitation didn't exist. In winter, most flies are crawling about the bottom of a stream in their nymphal stage. The black stone fly is an exception. May and June, when most nymphs come to the surface and molt, are when one traditionally catches trout on dry flies. As techniques and know-how have become more sophisticated, the dry fly season has been extended into September albeit with mostly teeny flies that no one much noticed before or was able to copy effectively. Still, artificial nymphs, wet flies, and other subsurface flies are commonly used in times other than May and June.

"I wanted to be able to go out on New Year's Day or the first of February or whatever, and be able to catch trout on a dry fly," Rick said. Rick had long been aware of the winter phenomenon of stone flies coming to the surface. However, the available dry stone fly imitations didn't work. "Over one winter, I just spent a lot of time watching the water," Rick said. "I saw that the trout ignored the artificials which sank a little. But they grabbed the naturals that just seemed to pop out of the water. My theory is that the water surface is so cold in winter, the emerging stone flies go into thermal shock, and want to dry their wings and get off as fast as possible. I experimented. Eventually, I found that reversing the hackle so the fly stood on the surface and also lacquering the wings were what was needed." Demand for Rick's fly at the nearby Sportsman's Den was such that forty dozen gross were sold within weeks. Now they're a regular winter item in the shop.

On a more playful note, Barry Serviente, of Carlisle, Pennsylvania, and some friends designed a fly to catch carp, generally a bottom-feeding, garbage-eating fish that lolls about turbid waters. Carp are one of the last fish a traditional fly-fisherman would aspire to catch. The setting was the Chesapeake & Ohio Canal that extends along the Potomac River from West Virginia into Washington, D.C. In the spring, the carp come to the surface, creating heart-stopping whorls in the water. They grab mulberries that fall from trees on the banks. The reader will guess what followed.

"We designed a mulberry fly," Barry said. "We used deer hair [which floats wonderfully] and mixed and matched until we got the right shade of red. We even had discussions on whether to add a stem." As artful as the mulberry fly was, the carp didn't always take it. "It wasn't so easy," Barry said. "But when it worked, it was super! A ten-pound carp is a strong fish, especially on a fly rod."

3

FIRST FISH ON A FLY

Without being especially conscious of what I was doing, I created the opportunity to catch a trout on a fly. The time was several years after the idyllic illustration of a fly-fisherman on the *Outdoor Life* cover had enchanted me. My dream was to fly-fish for trout. However, the means by which I would attain it were at best hazy. There was no assurance that what I wanted so much wouldn't remain forever a dream.

In the meantime, I'd begun hanging out at a sports shop that had a small area allocated to fly-fishing and, more important, two salesmen prepared to give some time to a boy with a lot of curiosity but little cash. There I confirmed and then supplemented the knowledge I'd derived from reading. In retrospect, the salesmen didn't know a whole lot themselves, but of course I didn't know that. They were my equivalent of Virgil leading Dante through the Inferno and then Purgatory to Heaven. To this day, five decades later, I recall a couple of their well-intentioned but rather unremarkable comments which, nonetheless, were for me wisdom to be treasured and, at the right occasion, put to good use.

"When fishing gets hard, I just switch to smaller and darker flies. Nine times out of ten, that works."

"Could you spot an ice cream cone across that street? Of course you could! The same way, trout can see a small fly."

I was a bit frightened by all they were telling me. I had trouble imagining using a fly at all, to say nothing of a small, dark fly that I'd have to manipulate so it floated naturally down rippling, always changing current without either drag or slack. Drag would occur from pulling in the line too hard, and slack from the opposite. I was soon to be put to the test.

The place was a quite special Boy Scout camp where I was a fourteen-year-old staff employee. The camp was in the mountains of the Shenandoah National Park in Virginia at the headwaters of the Rapidan River. It was built for President Hoover by the Marine Corps, principally as a retreat where he could fly-fish for trout and secondarily for informal meetings of state. Fate, if that's what it was, could hardly have done any better for me.

One day, leaning over the rail of a small footbridge across the Rapidan, ten feet wide at that point, I spotted the first trout I'd ever seen. They were six- or seven-inch elongated shapes, mostly holding in the clear current of the shallow, rock-strewn pool below. Occasionally, with a flick of their tails, the trout shifted gracefully a few inches to either side, evidently to snatch at something edible, visible only to them, drifting downstream. The proof that these shapes were trout was the thumping of my heart. My heart knew I was in the presence of my dream. Perch, blue gill, and other fish were just not fitting enough for such clear, cold, sun-mottled water; only trout could be here.

I returned to the bridge as often as my time permitted. I gazed at the fish, transfixed, becoming one of them as much as my imagination would allow. For me, these lithe, swift, water-borne creatures connoted a serenity that must be eternal and God-given. In another life, I'd want to be one of them. Perhaps I had been, or would be. Perhaps that was the origin of my attraction. Fishing was the best means of entering their world, albeit only momentarily.

At a weekend break between camp sessions, I went home with the first order of business to go, by trolley, to the sports store whence had come the only hands-on knowledge of fly-fishing I had. With the proceeds of my pay, I outfitted myself. It was a wonderful moment, choosing the tools I'd need to fulfill my dream.

First of all was the rod. It was a real cane rod, with two tips, made by a company called Montague. It cost all of $35, which is more remarkable when one understands that the price of most one-tip cane rods today begins at not much under $1,000. Those were the days of the three-cent postage stamp, but even when one factors in the current thirty-two-cent postage stamp as an inflation indicator, the price of a bottom-of-the-line cane rod has increased almost two and a half times. My rod warped and eventually the tips snapped, one in a car door, a common trap for cane rod tips, and the other, probably just from overuse, while I was casting. It was hardly the best of cane rods, but it lasted many years. (Cane rods can last several lifetimes, the quality of the cane being the determinant.)

The reel was a basic, cast metal Pflueger, a great choice, which survived four decades of battering. These reels are still made but are shunned by those who believe that expensive, hand-tooled reels will enable them to catch more fish. My line was silk. To prevent rot, it required greasing before use and drying afterward. Still, it didn't last long. The leaders were made of gut, just as they had been in Izaak Walton's time.

They required soaking to be pliable, but seemed more authentic and appropriate to this sport than the machine-extruded tapered nylon that soon followed.

The flies I purchased at a budget-busting 55 cents each were a few basic wet and dry Royal Coachmen, Black Gnats, Light Cahills, and Adams, all of them still good, conventional choices. There were a couple of other types then in vogue but now forgotten. If artificial nymphs were around then, I didn't know it, and streamers designed to imitate small fish were too large for my little stream. Tying my own flies was not an option I was aware of.

Next, it behooved me to make something of my investment. Spending my earnings on all this equipment, I'd taken a gamble that fly-fishing would be no more difficult than I'd been led to believe, and that I wouldn't be shamed, to say nothing of feeling myself a spendthrift, if it all came to naught. Nonetheless, the odds were with me. I felt, like the Biblical magi, that I was following, if not a heavenly light, an avocation that for me was as right as any could be.

My premonition was so correct that, strangely, I recall the place I caught my first trout, back on the Rapidan, but not the occasion or the fly I used. It all came as easily as water cascading quietly over rocks. My state-of-mind and study had assured success; luck was not a factor. Thus, no self-heroics or markings of the moment seemed to be called for.

In the time remaining for me in my job, I caught lots more trout, all of them very small. I caught them mostly on wet flies (flies designed to sink, which are easier to manage than dry flies) and it didn't seem to matter which flies I used. I also recall no difficulties in mastering the handling of fly rod and line although, because the stream was so small, only short casts were needed. Also, the hemlock trees that densely bordered the stream would have prevented a more demanding cast. Mostly, I caught trout on a downstream drift. That was easier than casting upstream and hauling in line neither faster nor slower than the fly floating downstream.

The trout were beautiful. They were brook trout, the trout

native to the eastern United States and Canada, and they were wild, which means they were born in the stream where they lived, not dumped there from a hatchery truck. In fact, there was no stocking of fish in the upper reaches of the Rapidan in those years. There are more clever varieties of trout that require more skill to catch, trout that are more exciting fighters and trout with subtler coloration. However, no fish of any kind is more spectacular than a stream-bred brook trout. Green and black squiggles cover their tops; on the sides are random spots of white with occasional spots of red surrounded by blue, and below, sometimes, there are yellow spots; the fins are orange with black and white borders, and their bellies are white. Described thus, the brook trout design seems a garish combination of conflicting color schemes, but it's not; one never tires marveling at freshly caught brook trout. Moreover, these fish change in color with seasons and different locations and, just as fascinating, no two are alike.

Rarely was I able to see trout in the Rapidan. From above, they are hard to distinguish from the rocks and gravel below them, except when they move, and they often hide under rocks, sunken logs, and undercut banks. The beauties I caught lived sometimes in water just a few inches deep. I traced the Rapidan up to its origins, where the water seeped cold out of springs somewhere under spongy moss covered ground or between rocks, and formed rivulets which gathered together to become the stream. I imagined where I, if I were a trout, would feel the securest and where I'd be close to food drifting downstream but not have to spend much energy staying in place, in short, where I'd be the happiest. I was able before long to anticipate their whereabouts.

The trout would dart from nowhere quick as an eye blink, and snatch the fly. Usually, I'd catch a flash of the fish's side. If not, I'd know of the strike because the shock would transmit itself instantly through the line to the rod and then my hand. After losing a few fish, the reflexes in my forearm became quick enough to strike back right away. These trout were so fierce in taking the fly that the hook usually was set firmly, and once hooked, a fish rarely escaped. The hooked trout would lunge about in a remarkable display of strength and agility before the bending but ultimately unforgiving power of the rod tired them. Holding the rod and line with one hand, I'd reach into the water with the other, grasp the fish, and then, with both hands, work the hook loose. I'd admire the fish a couple of seconds, and release it. It would be gone in another flash, vanished into the void from which it came. Its existence, then, became a memory, to be recalled as often as I wanted, especially in less perfect times when I needed the comfort of a reminder of the perfection of creation.

I was the only angler on the upper river. A few anglers probably fished the lower sections on weekends, but I never saw them. My half-dozen coworkers from the camp and the couple of adults who supervised us were not interested in fishing and, equally gratifying to me, in my fishing. I fished usually after dinner; dinner was early, and at that time of year, sundown was late. They had other things to do. I had the river to myself. There was no need to be aware even of the possibility of another person disturbing the water or me. An onlooker can make a novice, as I was then, self-conscious and even more awkward than normal. Alone, I was also able to concentrate on the swirls and eddies, and the direction by which they would carry my fly to the trout that might be lurking underneath. This dearth of competition also meant that the fish I caught almost certainly had never before seen an artificial fly.

The stream, within a two-and-a-half-hour drive of the nation's capital, is in the same condition now as it was then. So are the trout, thanks to conservation, enlightened regulation that prohibits the taking of trout, and tight government budgets. The latter have precluded improvements to the boulder-strewn access road, which remains impassable to all but high-carriage vehicles. The White House has taken back the camp, which is managed now by the Department of Interior for mostly second-level Executive Office officials. Presidents and cabinet officers usually go to Camp David in the Catoctin Mountains in Maryland. President Carter availed himself of trout fishing at both retreats and James Baker, Secretary of State under President Bush, is said to have fished the upper Rapidan. President Eisenhower seemed to prefer trout fishing in Western streams. President Bush was more of an open-water fisherman.

A couple of miles down the Rapidan is another camp, owned by a cooperative of several families. It was the original Hoover fishing camp. Following his inauguration in 1929, Hoover directed his staff to locate within one hundred miles of the White House a site for what, in effect, was to be his private fishing preserve. In those parts, it was commonly believed, the inhabitants were hillbilly subsistence farmers and moonshiners, this also being the time of Prohibition. Actually, the principal local product was tannin, and it caused more damage than bootleg whiskey. Leather is soaked in tannin to give it patina. The locals cut down the hemlock forests, stripping the trees of the bark, which they took to process. The trunks were left to rot. A few years later, when the national park was created, these folks were run off. Now, other than some gnarled remnants of orchards and a few fallen stone walls, there is little reminder of their hardscrabble lives.

According to legend, no one in the Hoover entourage thought of securing title to the property. All was well and good until one day the Secret Service arrested a trespassing bear hunter. He protested that the Secret Service agents were the ones who were trespassing; the property was his, he said. It was. The hunter was not a hillbilly but a prominent resident of the valley below. Moreover, he was a Democrat, as was just about everyone in the South then, and he was not an admirer of the President.

Hoover invited the landowner to the White House for a talk. It went badly. Hoover, supposedly a God-fearing Iowa Quaker, is said to have allowed to escape from his lips some ungodly sentiments. The matter went into litigation. In the meantime, Hoover had the camp moved upstream.

The ultimate presidential camp was built by five hundred Marines, with half this number remaining afterward to provide security. The project was billed as a training exercise for the Marines, although the cost of the land and some of the material was defrayed by the President.

A large number of rattlesnakes and copperheads were dislodged when the Marines blasted a road up the mountains and otherwise disrupted the landscape. Local hogs were brought in from nearby farms to rut out the snakes as a meal treat. Following construction, the hogs returned on their own in search of acorns and more snakes. The snakes by then had hidden themselves from both Marines and hogs. However, adding insult to injury, the Marines shot some of the disappointed hogs. Their owners were none too pleased, but were told, evidently, that they risked being shot themselves unless they stopped complaining and got off the property.

The President's physician, Vice Admiral Joel Boone, said, "I never saw him happier than when he was on the Rapidan. He could hardly wait to leave the car. He would go put on his rubber boots and hurry out to fish, seldom taking time to change from whatever he had been wearing." Indeed, pictures show Hoover fishing in Panama hat, high white collar and tie, suit jacket, hip boots, and creel. The stream was stocked with thousands of fish, many more than it could support, and varieties, including brown and rainbow trout, which are alien to that water. The result, the President angrily realized later, was that all the fish became stunted.

No one else was allowed to fish in the Rapidan without the permission of the Marine commanding officer. There was no fishing on the Sabbath and the season was short—April 1 to July 1—although the Virginia legislature empowered the fish commission to "provide such a season for trout fishing on the Rapidan as the President may desire."

Hoover himself said, "Next to prayer, fishing is the most . . . constant reminder of the democracy of life, of humility, and of human frailty—for all men are equal before fishes." However, in Hoover's value system, not all fish were equal. With some sarcasm, Hoover wrote of the "political potency" of fishing which induced his predecessors McKinley, Taft, Wilson, and Harding to take up the sport shared by many voters. Their prey was "common fishes," by which Hoover meant fish other than trout and salmon. Fly-fishing was without question the superior way to fish, and the only Presidents he credited as real fly-fishers were, besides himself, Theodore Roosevelt and Grover Cleveland.

In the nineteen-fifties, a cooperative movement headquartered in Roanoke, Virginia, was looking for an opportunity to develop a recreational co-op as a model for other such co-ops. Eventually, representatives stumbled over the original Hoover camp. The cabins were unlocked. They walked in one. In the semilight coming through small, dirty windows, they made out some dusty, mouse-chewed furniture, rusted appliances, and a light switch. They flicked the switch, and light came on. They walked to the adjacent room, a large kitchen, where they spotted a sink and water tap. They turned the tap, and water flowed. They were amazed. What they didn't know was that the aforementioned bear-hunting owner had kept the camp open for the convenience of other hunters. The co-op representatives made inquiries, met the landowner, and quickly completed what President Hoover had failed to do. They purchased the buildings and four acres on which they stand for $6,800. All that was required, seemingly, was some courtesy and, perhaps, the right political affiliation.

A couple of decades after the stream had recovered from the manipulations of the Hoover years, the state succumbed to pressure from angling thrill seekers to stock large rainbow trout. Because of their size, up to nineteen inches long, searching for these trout was exciting. However, in a mountain stream where native brook trout exceeding eleven inches were rarities, the big rainbows were doomed. They weakened, and were disappointing fighters. Moreover, with the possibility of coming across one of these giants, catching the more beautiful and feisty but smaller indigenous trout became, perversely, another disappointment. In addition, what few people, even conservationists, knew in those days was that stocked fish disrupt the feeding patterns of the natives.

Fish raised in wire-enclosed, concrete-bottomed hatcheries on processed food pellets have a harder time fending for themselves in natural environments. This sheltered upbringing becomes a handicap in the wild. Hatchery trout exhaust themselves as they aggressively displace the natives from choice feeding lanes and chase faraway prey. It's obvious to us now, although only recently have studies proving this been generally accepted.

"Catch and release" regulations for the Rapidan required returning all trout, including the big rainbows, to the stream, but the rainbows couldn't sustain themselves long enough to reproduce. The next idea was to stock even more fish and allow fishermen to keep their catch, a practice known as "put and take." The more enthusiastic proponents of this policy were the merchants in the valley, who decided the stream's renown could be turned into cash; the practice, they figured, would bring more fishermen to their shops and motels. The idea was quashed, and policy reverted to no stocking at all, fly-fishing only with barbless hooks with all fish to be released, unharmed. These are the current regulations, with the exception of the barbless hooks. Fisheries research has found that the mortality rates of fish caught on barbless hooks and released are little different from those of fish caught on barbed hooks.

An old-timer told me that prior to the creation of the national park, when runoff from the mountainside farms washed garbage into the Rapidan, fishing was better. Now, without domestic nutrients, stocking, and other manipulation, the Rapidan sustains a relatively large population of wild trout (fifty pounds per acre of water, as measured by the Virginia fisheries conservationists). Fishing in the upper Rapidan now is the way nature intended it to be. It's probably no different than it was when I caught my first trout there nearly half a century ago and, indeed, before the first man ever saw the stream. The fish aren't large but they're beautiful and lively.

Coming full circle, one of the family members of the Rapidan cooperative is mine. My son, Peter, uttered his first word there, "rain," almost twenty-five years ago. He was tuned into a combination of incessant pattering of rain on the roof and complaints about the weather by cabin-bound adults one spring weekend. In any event, our easy access to the stream is assured for as long as the camp remains, which should be at least through my children's lifetimes.

4

DOROTHEA AND HER FRIENDS

I n the balmiest, most pleasant and intoxicating two weeks of spring, Dorothy appears, usually at dusk, fairylike, dressed in pale yellow. She dances in the air above trout streams in strange, high vertical rises and falls. She drives the trout crazy, and the trout, in turn, drive fly-fishers crazy. Dorothy and her aquatic insect cousins are the principal diet of most trout.

Dorothy's real name is *Ephemerella dorothea. Ephemerella* is the family name; in the insect world, family and given names are reversed from ours. Dorothy's family is one of eighty members of a larger family, which in turn is one of five hundred belonging to the *Ephemeroptera* family. The name derives from the Greek *ephemera,* meaning lasting a brief time, transient, and maybe even a bit tragic. Dorothy has a plain English name, which is Pale Evening Dun. She also has some aliases including Pale Watery Dun, Yellow May, Sulphur Dun, and Little Sulphur Dun. Pale Morning Dun is someone else (known in Latin as *Ephemerella inermis*), although to the uninitiated, she looks virtually the same as Pale Evening Dun. Pale Morning Dun lives more in the western United States. Dorothy and her ephemeral relatives are known collectively as mayflies.

Dorothy's life span is two years. However, she's beautiful for only two days, her last. The rest of the time, she's an ugly ten-segmented, six-legged, three-tailed nymph with large pincers for a mouth. In this form, she mucks about rocks and mud in the bottom of her stream, staying out of the way of the trout as best she can. The trout love her, not for her looks, of course, but for her food value; on a nutritional scale, she's more packed with protein, calories, minerals, and vitamins than even bait fish. Even the largest trout can live entirely on aquatic insects.

Dorothy's whole life is directed at these two last days. In a way, it's about love. She doesn't even eat. In her finest garb, she attracts a mate, procreates, drops her eggs into the stream, and then, her purpose served, dies. Ironically, once dead, her clear, sparkly, and still beautiful wings spread vertically on the stream surface, she's of much less interest to trout. Her food value has been pretty well spent.

Dorothy's eggs sink slowly to the stream's bottom, finding crevices between stones where they nestle. In a couple of weeks, they hatch into tiny, almost invisible nymphs, which are food for fish, ducks, dragon fly larvae, hellgrammites, and other aquatic predators. They also are killed by pesticides and a dearth of oxygen, one of the effects of pollution. Those nymphs that survive are hungry. They draw oxygen from the water through a series of gills. The nymphs feed on algae, to the extent that they can keep a stream clear of it, and plankton, minute animal and plant life that drift or swim in the currents. When the nymphs grow too large for their outermost waxy layer of skin, they split the top layer, break out, and grow a new skin. Because they have no backbone and only their outer skin, called exoskeleton, as support, molting is especially difficult. Molting occurs several dozen times until the nymphs are fully grown. During this entire time, trout seek out the nymphs and, in turn, may be caught on nymph imitations, even in winter where winter fishing is permitted. Obviously, all but a small portion of trout feeding is beneath the water surface, out of sight of fishermen.

When the nymphs are mature, they grow wing cases on their backs. They become particularly restless, even traveling to the surface from time to time for a look-see, and then returning to the bottom of the stream. They lose some of their normal caution, and in the process some lose their lives to alert trout.

Inside their nymphal skins, they generate gasses that help them rise like a buoy to within five to ten inches of the surface. There, at the end of their nymphal stage and when the water temperature tells them it's time to move on, they move the rest of the way to the surface, struggle to break through the surface film, and once on top, split their skin along their back for the last time, and climb out. All of a sudden, they are no longer mottled brown nymphs with gills and jaws, but mayflies with four dull wings, three thin tails, and a yellow body. They have no jaws with which to eat. They unfold and dry their wings. This process, for the *Ephemerella dorothea,* occurs in the late afternoon and early evening, unless the water is discolored or the sky is cloudy, in which cases their instincts may be fooled and they rise earlier. Probably, generations of selective breeding have told the *Ephemerella dorothea* that, in dimming light, they'll be less susceptible to another predator—birds.

In this second stage, aquatic insects are called duns, because of their dull color. As their wings dry, the duns test them with occasional flutters. Their time floating on the surface, sometimes using their discarded skins as a sort of a raft, lasts a half minute to a minute, and takes them thirty to fifty feet downstream. During this time, they're especially vulnerable, and the trout attack them with abandon.

As soon as the *Ephemerella dorothea* duns are able, they escape the water and fly somewhat clumsily, to a nearby bush or tree. In the process, some are picked off by swallows, swifts, phoebes, night hawks, and other birds and, later, bats swooping over the stream. Those that survive long enough to fly to a bush or tree cling to the protected undersides of leaves or their stems. In a few hours, they undergo still another metamorphosis, developing breeding organs. They also change shape again, growing more slender with greatly enlarged tails and more powerful wings. Their body colors brighten, and their wings become translucent. In this, their last stage, they're sometimes called spinners.

The spinners take to the air in swarms above the stream, rising on rapidly beating wings as much as forty-five feet and then descending, wings outstretched like parachutes, to ten feet from the surface. While difficult to catch now, the swarms attract birds and bats again, in even greater numbers. Male spinners synchronize their flight with that of the females, and on the rise, attach themselves to the thoraxal undersides of the females. They copulate in flight, with the female carrying the male. Once her eggs are fertilized, he drops off and rejoins the swarm to mate again. She flutters down to the stream, a few yards above the point where she emerged as a dun, and drops her egg sac into a slow-moving section of current, or allows the surface tension of the water to pull off the sac. She rejoins the swarm, but eventually weakens and falls, exhausted, into the water or nearby shore.

Besides mayflies, trout and other insect-eating fish feed on what are called stoneflies, caddis flies, sedges, and two-winged creatures like craneflies, midges, and gnats. In midsummer, they also feed on terrestrial insects such as ants, grasshoppers, leafhoppers, and beetles, and occasionally winged terrestrials such as bees and wasps. Other aquatic trout food includes scuds, erroneously known as freshwater shrimp, and sowbugs. None of these creatures sounds appetizing to us, but the trout love them and fly-fishermen are tireless in creating their imitations.

The basic materials for tying artificial flies are feathers, fur, silk, and some artificial yarns. Each of the components of the artificial fly—wings, body, legs, and tails—requires a different material. Sounds simple, maybe, but the process of selecting the most suitable materials can become enormously complex and compelling. Let's take a look at Dorothy, or her common name, the Pale Evening Dun, as seen by three fly tiers, in the late nineteenth century, early twentieth century, and now.

The first tier, Alfred Ronalds, an Englishman, recommended early in the nineteenth century, the following:

> Wings: From a very fine grained feather of the starling's
>   wing stained of rather a lighter yellow . . .
> Body: Yellow martin's fur spun on pale fawn-coloured
>   silk thread.
> Legs: Pale dun hackle.

Mr. Ronalds suggested as alternative for the legs which, if obtainable, apparently was preferable:

> The hair of an abortive calf, which would have been red
> if born at the proper time, is a resplendent gold colour,
> and forms a good material for the legs of Summer duns.

In 1935, in the first American book that combined fly dressings, as they're sometimes called, with accurate descriptions of the insects they represent, Preston Jennings suggested:

> Wings: Palest starling.
> Body: Fur from the flank of an Australian opossum.
> Legs: Pale ginger cock.
> Tails: Ginger cock barbs.
> Silk: Primrose.

Eric Leiser, modern-day sage on the subject and author of several fly-tying books, is more practical.

Wings: Light blue hackle tip.
Tails: Light blue dun hackle fibers.
Body: Pale yellow dubbing fur.
Hackle: Light blue dun.
Thread: Cream or primrose.

The three Pale Evening Duns are not that different from each other, except that now legs are called hackle and are used more to support a dry fly on the surface of the water than to resemble legs. Hackle is a piece of feather wrapped around the hook in a circle. Moreover, Mr. Leiser's materials are less specific than those cited by the earlier two tiers, Mr. Leiser believing that dyed fur and feathers from domestic hens are entirely acceptable. Mr. Leiser adds, somewhat euphemistically, "There are forty recipes now for the Pale Evening Dun."

Mr. Leiser has instructions for tying Pale Evening Dun dry fly counterparts in wet fly, nymph, and parachute (a dry fly variety) patterns. For the nymph, he uses two kinds of duck wings (wood duck and mallard) and brown partridge hackle as well as some fine gold wire to delineate the rib sections.

Most fly tiers are constantly watching for "road kill"—rabbit, opossum, woodchucks, squirrel, deer, and birds of all kinds. Parts of virtually anything that walks or flies can be used as fly-tying material. Some fly tiers snoop around sheep ranches for fur from the underparts of rams, and others around ranges where wood ducks, the feathers of which are especially precious, are shot. Imported materials such as the aforementioned Australian opossum fur are hard to come by today, and except for three kinds of pheasant and the pea hen, the U.S. government, in an effort to encourage other countries to protect their wild birds, prohibits the import of feathers for sale. Feathers from wild birds in this country also may not be commercially sold, although they may be bred domestically for sale. A century ago, egrets were nearly wiped out by hunters in the Everglades, who shot them by the thousands while they were nesting with their young, the one time in their life cycle when they are vulnerable. The commercial market that generated the slaughter was created by milliners, who used the plumes in women's hats. Some milliners added a special style touch with beaks and claws, and sometimes constructed hats from whole birds. The killing stopped only when there weren't enough birds left to justify the hunters' efforts.

The ban in the United States includes highly valued feathers from the jungle cock in India, which nicely imitate the eyes of bait fish; the toucan from Central America, with their especially fine textures as well as astonishing colors; gray condors from South America; florican bustards from Asia; the Kenya crested guinea fowl; the African gray parrot, and the scarlet ibis of the Caribbean. Some of the brighter, more exotic feathers were included in salmon flies, which used to be tied more to please the human eye than to attract fish. Or perhaps the tiers thought the two were the same. To this day, no one is sure why salmon strike these bright flies other than, perhaps, irritation or maybe a memory of gorging on insects from their early days; when they return to fresh water, they don't need to eat.

Most feathers used in fly tying these days are from domestic fowl bred for the purpose. The best rooster necks and saddles cost, at most recent prices, $85. One is advertised as follows: "The barb count and stiffness are the highest on the market. The quill—the most critical part—of each feather is flexible, thin and long." The same producer claims that feathers from its saddles average six inches in length, and compared to an average of four to five flies per feather, one of its feathers is sufficient to produce three hundred flies. That might well justify the expense. Contemporary fly tiers also needn't muck about barn yards, peer into roadside ditches, or even hunt animals for fur for fly bodies. These, too, are provided commercially. One can buy chunks of hair of bull elk, yearling elk, caribou, moose (manes), muskrats (bellies), black bear, mongoose, martins, minks, badger, beaver, English hares (ears), and gray fox.

Machine-made materials such as mylar, acrylic, and antron are finding their way into fly construction. Their inventors give others great names like Krystal Flash, Lite Brite, Glo Bug, Twinkle, Bobby Dazzle, and Flashabou. Some of these materials reflect light in a way the naturals do not, and on occasion are especially provocative to trout. However, no man-made materials match feathers and fur for buoyancy, stiffness, and durability. For most fly-fishers, who tend by nature to be traditionalists, that's a comfort. Dorothy may be pleased, too, that her imitations are likely to remain substantially the same as those of her ancestors.

5

THE PERILS

The perils of fly-fishing are many, and are not to be taken lightly. Every fly-fisherman must deal with them. Only the truly committed survive to continue fishing. The perils are that bad. Any one can extinguish a novice's interest in fly-fishing.

If attracted to fly-fishing by the opportunity to imitate a character in *A River Runs Through It,* or to wear a new cool-looking fly-fishing outfit, or to be able to impress people with a fly-fishing story or two, chances are that the angler will soon decide that mosquitoes, cold toes, tangled leaders, and the like just aren't worth the image. Surviving the perils can be considered a definition of commitment. If an angler continues to fly-fish after a season or two, it's likely that his motivations are basic, God-given, and real, and that he will overcome the frustrations intrinsic to the sport.

"No more, enough, that's it, I'm through!" Virtually every fly-fisher has expressed this sentiment. When this occurs, the energy that once went into fly-fishing will be channeled to boxing, shell collecting, motorcycle racing, Old Testament study, or some other avocation. However, if fishing is a basic enough component of the angler's mental makeup, he or she eventually will be drawn back to fly-fishing.

Let's review the perils, or at least the most obvious ones.

NO FISH.

This is certainly the number one turn off. Fishermen are results oriented. Results mean fish—in the net or maybe lost after having been hooked, or still acceptable for some, enticed either to swat the fly or to move out of its feeding lane in the current to examine it. A smaller number of fishermen are content just to be on the water. The latter tend to be veteran anglers with enough memories of good catches to be confident that good fishing will recur in due course.

Even the rare fishermen happy just to be in the water must have some evidence of fish. In the case of salmon, knowledge of their proximity may be enough, even if this means the salmon are miles downstream but reported to be showing an inclination to move upstream. (Salmon can swim thirty miles up-current in a night.) Fishing in water one knows to be void of fish isn't fishing. It may be practicing fishing, or pretending to fish, or having a nice day, but it's not fishing. Even the more experienced, confident, patient, and optimistic fishermen would prefer catching fish than not.

Less-experienced fishermen usually need encouragement. Assurance that their fishing technique is improving will suffice for a while but not forever. At some point, they need to catch fish. Otherwise, disappointment sets in. This is a hazard, as fishless days are not uncommon for even the best of fishermen in the best of waters. Sometimes, there is just nothing that can be done to induce fish to strike. Strictly speaking, fishless days are evidence of failure. The capacity to tolerate them must be learned. It requires a disciplined long-term, big-picture perspective on life as well as fishing. It's not easy, and some beginning fishermen are lost to the sport along the way.

The anticipation of catching fish used to be so great for me that adrenaline would start to flow long before I even entered the water. The bad side was the disappointment that would follow if I caught nothing. I'm more relaxed now, albeit far from entirely so. My heartbeat still quickens as I approach fishing water.

BAD CONDITIONS.

These include:

Wrong water temperature. Fish feed normally only in a certain band of temperature. Their body being the same temperature as the water that surrounds them, their temperature is more variable than ours, and temperature changes affect their behavior more radically. If water temperatures are too low, their metabolism renders them sluggish and they don't feed much. If temperatures are too high, their metabolism will cause them to expend more energy moving to feed than they'll gain by feeding. Therefore, they don't move or feed much when water temperatures are much warmer or colder than optimum.

Different fish have different temperature sensitivities. The ideal range for trout is between fifty-four and sixty-four degrees. This varies within the trout family itself. Brook trout, for example, are the least tolerant of warm water. The lethal high for trout is about seventy-seven degrees, although some acclimatized trout may live for short periods in warmer water. American grayling need even colder water to survive. At the warm end of the scale among fresh water game fish are black bass, but even within that family there are differences. Small-mouth black bass live in Maine while their largemouth cousins are happier in Florida.

The life cycles of aquatic insects are also keyed to water temperatures, causing still another variable to frustrate fly-fishermen. Changes from temperature norms can disrupt the hatch times fishermen expect from their logs of previous fishing trips (a few highly organized anglers actually keep these) or insect hatch charts.

Aware of this difficulty, many serious fly-fishermen add thermometers to the array of paraphernalia they carry around. Fly shops near streams, as a service to their customers, sometimes report stream temperatures. Nonetheless, even within the same body of water, there are temperature differences. Water near spring holes and feeder streams is colder in warm weather. Trout tend to congregate at these spots to escape heat, except maybe at night when they may make food-finding forages into the main currents. More serious local trout fishermen find these cold spots. Water temperatures also change during the day, enough usually to make a difference in fishing. Early or late in the season trout are more active midday, when the water is briefly warmed by the sun. Generally, water temperature changes can be predicted by air temperature, but not always. For example, in the spring, melting snow can cause water temperatures to drop to near freezing, ruining what may have been reasonably good fishing only hours earlier. Conversely, heavy rain in midsummer can quickly improve fishing.

Water level. Water can be too high or too low. If it's too high, owing to rain or snow melts, instinct tells fish that the amount of energy required to come to the now higher surface through stronger current isn't worth the effort. At the same time, the fisherman may not be able to get a lure near the fish. On the other hand, if there isn't enough water, the fish will be spooky, feeling more vulnerable to predators—ospreys, hawks, and eagles; fish-eating animals such as otters; other fish, including pike; and fishermen. They tend to find a dark, quiet spot, hunker down, and stay still, except maybe at night when they feel safer. Either way, the fisherman is out of luck, or at best finds his fish-catching chances diminished.

Murky water. This peril can ruin a good day's fishing as surely as any of the others. Rain or snow runoff, nearby construction, or a lot of power boats churning about on a lake, can pour earthly detritus into the water or stir up the bottom. Whatever the cause, fish have trouble in murky water seeing, smelling, or sensing the movement of food or what they think might be food, including fishing lures. Murky water can be an unpleasant surprise upon arriving at a stream after a drive from home of several hours or even a day or two. However, it's a surprise virtually every longtime fly-fisher has faced.

Bright light. Fish feel more vulnerable when the light is unusually bright, such as at midday in midsummer. More important, however, is the effect of light on aquatic insects. They need to retain a certain amount of moisture in their systems to stay alive for the two or three days they're in the air during their mating cycle. An instinctual fear of dehydration will keep them below, frustrating the fisherman's anticipation of a hatch in what otherwise may be ideal conditions.

WRONG FLIES.

There are times, especially during a heavy hatch, when trout are even more selective than normal. To have a reasonable chance of a strike, the fisherman must have a near exact imitation. This includes the insect's life stage (maybe, if the spinners are falling, it's too late for the duns), size (when a #14 hook is right, a #12 or #16 won't do), and color (a pale yellow body may be what's called for rather than off-white, or vice versa). Sometimes, there may be so many naturals around, even a good imitation won't attract fish. To make matters worse, while the fisherman is unaware, the life stage of the insect may change or the hatch of another insect may claim the attention of the fish.

Even good fishermen find themselves without the right flies from time to time, especially in areas that are new to them. Most experienced fishermen can at least identify the nature of the problem. However, for inexperienced fishermen, especially when the fish are actively and visibly feeding, the problem can be discouraging.

WRONG EQUIPMENT.

Even the most experienced anglers have found upon arriving at a remote stream that they've left a reel or some other crucial item at home. Also, with bad information, the fisherman may find that conditions call for a heavier or lighter rod, or sinking line when floating line is what they have, or the other way around. This leads to the next peril.

BAD ADVICE.

Fishing is an exercise in faith. No matter how elaborate the fisherman's preparations, there is no assurance that he will catch anything. Too many unknowns are present. Water temperatures, hatches, and a myriad of other factors are simply unpredictable. In an extension of the faith the fisherman demonstrates in deciding to fish in the first place, he is prone to accept advice, even if it's unsolicited and of uncertain soundness.

The authority of the advisor is rarely questioned, especially if he or she speaks without hesitation and in a loud voice. Often the advice taker bestows authority on the advice giver solely because the giver has fished the same water more recently or more frequently. This isn't necessarily wrong. However, the faith that prevails in fishing is so great that most fishermen tend to set aside natural skepticism and forget that no one has all the answers.

Hence, the advice seeker may be told:

1. "The last week in September is our best time. It's right before the cold sets in, and the salmon are always running then. Come on up!"
2. "Do you have any Matukas? They're really fantastic! Green works best."
3. "Conditions are about perfect. Water temperature was fifty-five this morning, flow is at eighteen hundred cubic feet, and the Hendrickson hatch is at its peak."

The principal danger of all three hypothetical, ostensibly helpful items of advice is that conditions may change, and change too late for the fisherman to cancel his trip, stay at home, play with the children, mow the lawn, or otherwise do something more useful than flail water with a fly line. In Item 1, the setting being a salmon fishing camp in Canada, the angler also may have had to commit to spending quite a lot of money on transportation, lodging, meals, license, and guides. In Item 2, a green Matuka may work better, as well as, or worse than another streamer. Probably, there's no difference. If the advice giver uses nothing but green Matukas and occasionally catches fish, of course he can certify that they work. Furthermore, Matukas could have worked for him on Day 1, but on Day 2, when the advice seeker is on the stream, the trout may be looking for something entirely different. The problem with Item 3 is the same as with Item 1: conditions may have changed.

TOO MUCH ADVICE.

Let's say that you want to fish the Housatonic River in northwestern Connecticut, one of the finest public trout rivers in the East, and you've chosen the last week in May, the peak season for fly hatches. You go into Phil Dimitri's fly shop for advice.

"Well," he says, "what's been coming off are . . . Here, take a look in the jar. That's them; there's a . . . and a . . . , and that one you see at the top of the glass is the . . . The guys also tell me they've been having luck on . . . Are you planning to be around for the evening hatch? . . . OK, you'll want to have some . . . and some . . . and some . . . and right at dark . . . work best. Midday is tough, but you'll find them sipping on . . . and of course, under the surface they'll be taking . . . and . . . Are you going to spend the night and fish the early rises? This morning one of the fellows said he took a . . . -inch trout from Two-Car Hole on a . . ." And so it goes.

What Phil tells you that you need in order to cover all the bases on this particular day are: March Browns, sizes 10 and 12; Gray Foxes, size 14; Light Cahills, sizes 16 and 18; Sulphurs, sizes 16 and 18; Green Caddis flies, sizes 16 and 18; Black Caddis flies (which are just starting), sizes 18 and 20; Giant Black Stone flies, size 6 or 8; Crane flies, size 16 in a pale cream; Brown Drakes, sizes 10 and 12; the midge Ephemerella Needhami, sizes 22 and 24; and Baetis, which is another midge, size 22. These are in dry fly patterns. You should have the nymph patterns of each as well. The nymphs are useful all day, whereas the caddis are more morning flies and the mayflies more evening flies. These flies won't all be hatching together, but there will be substantial overlap. Other rivers and streams are similar in terms of insect hatches although not many are as prolific.

To demonstrate, Phil will show you the real flies. He's caught them that day, and you'll see them fluttering in a glass jar, or if you and he happen to be outside, he may point out others blown from the nearby river and trapped in a spider web in the corner of the shop's front window. Call it, if you will, hands-on entomology. In any event, you'll have no question about what you'll want to imitate.

Now Phil, who lives on the water and knows what to expect

and when, will be able to discern the different patterns almost as well as the trout. However, without checking a chart (hatches occur pretty much the same times every year), most fisherfolk won't be sure what to use. Moreover, possessing each of the patterns listed above for this particular week in May in each of the right sizes can cause confusion; they're just too many. Owning a great number of flies can lead to over-frequent changes of flies, which of course means less time fishing. At the same time, it can deplete the purse and clutter the fly box. I go crazy sometimes sorting among flies I can no longer identify or recall why I bought them. The fly-fisher's temptation is to be fully prepared, but is it worth the effort? The answer depends upon the fly-fisher's expertise in identifying hatches and, accordingly, in avoiding confusion. The greater the abundance of hatches, however, the greater the peril.

INFORMATION OVERLOAD.

Related to an excess of advice is an excess of information. Books on fly-fishing are tumbling off the presses in incredible numbers. Nick Lyons, a publisher of some of the better ones, estimates that five hundred titles are currently in print in English. More will come. The books cover every conceivable subject and some that are not conceivable. Not only are hundreds of books written on tying flies, many of them with fine drawings and gorgeous color plates, but there are books on tiers of flies and one on a family of fly tiers. Writers compete with each other for the publication of the most exhaustive compendia of information of aquatic insect species tasty to trout. Books describe fly-fishing for panfish, hardly a test of skill or wits; sunfish, blue gill, perch, and their ilk are not particularly discriminating in what they ingest. Chances are that if your favorite fishing water is large enough, someone has written a brochure if not a book on it, perhaps with diagrams of how to fish each hole. More than one hundred different magazines or brochures on fly-fishing are shoved into mail slots every month.

The testing of writers' creativity becomes more onerous. With so much having been written on the subject, originality often means narrowing an existing focus. Scientific studies are obvious sources of massive data on small subjects, but efforts are made to write about somewhat more popular subjects, some of which may be surprising or even interesting, assuming, of course, one has time to read them. One magazine published an article entitled "Understanding Deer Hair." Deer hair is a fly-tying staple because of its remarkable ability to keep flies afloat. However, there are different kinds of deer, some parts of the deer provide better hair than others, and the hair changes, too, with the seasons.

Then there are the catalogs. If budding or falling leaves or even a slight lengthening in the light of the day don't remind one of an impending change in the season, fishing equipment catalogs will. The catalogs show up as sure as the seasons change, every time, seemingly, with more pages, better color and artwork, and heavier, better stock. Some of them even carry a price tag of several dollars.

Concurrent with book, magazine, and catalog publication is the propagation of videos promising either armchair adventure or information, including fly-fishing techniques the viewer is led to believe are essential to fishing success and, by implication, satisfaction with life. In addition, to entertain us at fly-fishing club meetings and dinners are speakers, some of whom, despite fees that reach into four figures for an evening, are booked more than a year in advance.

This plethora of information covers aquatic entomology and ichthyology as well as fly-fishing techniques. Much is innovative. It's a result of increasingly sophisticated studies at universities and state fishery departments, and by equipment manufacturers and students writing Ph.D. dissertations. Some of it is interesting to fly-fishers, and some of it is even useful. However, there is no way any longer that ordinary mortals can even hope to keep up with the fly-fishing data explosion. That, by itself, is still another frustration inherent in the sport.

HIGH COSTS.

Not only can flies be expensive, but so is just about everything else associated with fly-fishing. The $2 (plus or minus) cost of an ordinary trout fly may not seem like much until one realizes how many flies one is induced to buy from store display cases or catalog, and how easily they're lost on bushes, submerged logs, rocks, and occasionally, fish. At the high end of the cost scale are exotic fishing trips; the price tag for a week's fishing rights on a salmon beat at the height of the season on the Alta River in Norway is $20,000. In addition to the basic rod, reel, line, and boots, all of which can be ferociously expensive, is specially designed clothing for the fashion conscious. Tying one's own flies can be even more expensive than buying them ready-made. A good neck of feathers for tying dry fly hackles from a specially bred rooster costs as much as $85. Worms, too, which in early spring are hard to find in the backyard, are available commercially, at a price.

BUGS.

Here we're talking about the earthly kind that like to chew on people—especially mosquitoes, black flies, deer flies, and horse flies. If peril is too strong a word, biting bugs are certainly a detriment to fishing pleasure, and can discourage all but the most determined fishermen. When the peaceful aquatic flies (which don't feed at all when outside the water) are most prolific, so are their terrestrial people-biting cousins.

OTHER PEOPLE.

The novice fisherman seeking the solitude that's often associated with fly-fishing may be sorely disappointed. There are few streams within a couple of hours' drive from urban centers in the United States that aren't host to other fishermen, and often a lot of them, except maybe toward the end of the season when most other fishermen become bored or believe, usually mistakenly, that no fish are left. At worst, one competes for streamside space with other fishermen, fearful, rightly or wrongly, that they will put down whatever fish happen to be around or snag one's line. Muttering and occasionally insults and even threats by more territorial fishermen in such situations are far from unknown. What prevents actual combat in such situations usually is the water between the disputants which would have to be crossed in waders in ungainly, undignified fashion, probably provoking laughter.

My largest catch on a fly was a one hundred and seventy-pound dentist. He and a companion saw from the commotion made by the small group I was with that we were into a concentration of steelhead trout, a variety of rainbow trout that migrates like salmon to and from the sea or large lakes and become large. The pair approached us from behind. My territorial instincts took hold and I semiconsciously extended my back casts until, sure enough, I hooked him—in the ear. Now fully aware of what I'd done, and why, I was ashamed and also a bit horrified. I apologized. "No problem," the dentist said. He semiconsciously understood that he was trespassing into our territory, and he was ready, apparently, to suffer any reasonable consequences. As his companion had a pair of wire cutters in his vest and there are few nerves in the outer ear, the consequences were minor.

Also unnerving is the following not uncommon situation. To your surprise, you discover in some unlikely, out-of-the-way place a pool where you enjoy not only solitude but also unusually good fishing. There's no evidence by way of footprints, paths, empty Styrofoam bait cartons, beer cans, strands of broken leader attached to bushes, or other trash that anyone else fishes there. You feel crafty and wise, proud of the acumen that led you to the spot. Perhaps you mention it to a few others, but if so, in veiled terms that avoid specifying the location. You anticipate fishing there in the future, picturing just where you'll stand in the pool and the spots to which you'll cast, and planning strategy, including choice of flies. You hear in your mind the songs of the birds that will be there, imagine the breeze on your face, and picture the intensity and direction of light at the time of day you expect to be there. Getting to the hole takes time. Perhaps it even includes a hike with equipment on your back through dense woods where the branches claw at your arms and legs. You arrive, finally. Someone else got there before you. In fact, he's exactly where you would have been, if only you'd been there first. He's casting to the same spots you'd be casting. There's no room for two, or maybe there is but the thought of sharing the pool now is too much to bear. The disappointment can amount to outrage.

Of course, those were my experiences. I've found unspoiled, seemingly untouched spots with wild trout within a forty-mile radius of Manhattan, only to have them discovered by others. The disappointment is acute but, with increasing numbers of anglers, inevitable. I'm forced to creep deeper into the woods in search of new spots, or return to the old spots at unusual hours such as nightfall or the middle of a workday.

6

FISHING WITH SPOUSE

S ince Cleopatra's time, and probably earlier, women have fished for sport. Some, like Dame Juliana, have written on the subject, and women's fishing clubs have been around for at least sixty years. However, until recently, the number of women anglers and fishing couples has not been large.

In America, fishing used to be an almost exclusively male domain. Women were expected to have other interests. The retreats built by the wealthy in the northeastern United States in the nineteenth century had club houses with common sleeping and bathing quarters, obviously for men only. To make matters crystal clear, the bylaws of many specified that membership was limited to men. For the club founders, fishing was a time-tested, accepted, no-questions-asked means to escape from the tribulations of dealing with the other sex, al-

ways a difficult proposition, even in that time of male domi-
nance. For some men, fishing trips were not especially for fishing; many were there to play cards, shoot the breeze, and
enjoy all-male conviviality. If the man was sufficiently affluent
and needing of a break from spousal and familial duties, these
trips could last for several months. One Buffalo, New York, in-
dustrialist used to bring his wife, children, other relations, and
servants by private rail car to a "camp" in the Adirondacks that
included a lodge with rooms for twenty family members and
guests, separate guest house, boat house, laundry house, guide
house for the resident male staff, and other outbuildings. The
camp fronted a lake with reasonably good trout fishing. However, after a few days, the patriarch would absent himself to
still another camp, in Canada, built in the same style as the
first but more rustic, where he'd fish for salmon for a few
weeks. This pattern wasn't uncommon in those circles. Of
course, it was entirely likely that some of the wives welcomed
the annual separation; they may have needed a break as well.

More often than not, women didn't have time even to
think about fishing; managing a household was virtually a
twenty-four-hour-a-day occupation. As gender boundaries
began to crumble, starting with expectations of women's ca-
pabilities and extending into education and then the profes-
sions, the time they had to pursue other activities expanded.
Similarly, barriers to fishing began to fall.

Now, women are encouraged to fly-fish by a vast and growing sports equipment industry which produces waders, vests,
clothing, and accessories designed specifically for women.
The accessories include silk scarves and bandannas that can
be retied in a "fancy knot" suitable for "après-fishing cock-
tails," and polarized sunglasses in a "classic cat-eye design,
sized to frame, not overpower, a woman's face." Colors may
be "environmentally friendly" to fit into surroundings, com-
plement each other when "layered," and "give a touch of fem-
ininity" on a trout stream. The move to fashion in fishing is
all the more poignant when one realizes that the first fishing
vest was designed not so long ago by Lee Wulff (perhaps the

foremost student, instructor, and practitioner of fly-fishing of our times), who sewed some extra pockets on an old shirt and cut off the sleeves. Further encouragement springs from travel agents who specialize in fishing in exotic places; fishing lodges that welcome women; guides, some of whom are women; fishing schools, some managed and taught by women; and fishing books written by and for women.

This commercial exploitation of the women's fly-fishing market eventually "will subside to a dull roar," comments Silvio Calabi, vice president of the Downeast Outdoor Group, Rockport, Maine, publishers of fishing and hunting books and magazines. The reason, Mr. Calabi thinks, is, "When women catch up with men—not only in angling skills but also in being accepted on-stream—they will neither want nor need special treatment." Equipment modifications for women, of course, will remain. "Why should a woman wear cut-down men's waders, or have to buy a five hundred–dollar rod the handle of which is shaped to a man's hands?" he asks.

"Fly-fishing is a great sport for women," Mr. Calabi adds. "Brute strength doesn't play a big part. What's needed—balance, agility, coordination, patience—a lot of women have."

However, women still don't fish in nearly the proportions as men. One may ask why. An explanation may be that while differences between the sexes are not as significant as was supposed in the nineteenth century, they do exist. In general, men may derive more satisfaction from fishing than women. If this is true, perhaps the reason is that an instinct to hunt was bred hundreds of thousands of years ago in men to a greater extent than in women. Be that as it may, many women seem to have the same instinct, albeit in degrees varying from that of the most avid male hunter or fisher to virtually nil.

Joan Wulff, the widow of Lee Wulff, concurs. Mrs. Wulff is renowned in her own right as a writer, a champion fly caster, and the proprietor/manager of a fly-fishing school.

"Women are the products of two parents," she says. "The predator instinct may be there but buried. Just look around the office. Some of the women clearly are predators, sometimes more so than men. Women can listen for this instinct, develop it, and use it. But men are more likely to have it. For example, men are more likely to be able to read water and just know where the fish are."

To the extent this instinct exists in a woman, it can provide a bridge to men. For my wife, Denise, fishing led to marriage.

One fine Sunday in early spring at the beginning of our courtship, I offered Denise, who I knew felt most at home in the concrete canyons of New York City, a choice of activities that included fishing. Out of curiosity, and from some ignorance of what was to follow, Denise chose the fishing option. We bought a license and drove to the local trout stream. Denise pulled on a pair of hip waders, the bulk and awkwardness of which were like nothing she had ever experienced. I provided some rudimentary instruction on the use of a fly rod and how to throw out enough line to allow a somewhat natural downstream float.

What was even more bizarre, Denise told me later, was the feel of the uneven, slippery, shifting rock bottom of the stream, and the force of the water rushing between her legs. For me, the feeling was entirely natural; I'd spent a significant part of my life in waders. Seeing that Denise needed some time to become accustomed to this environment, I suggested that she wade back to land and meet me downstream one hundred yards, passing another fisherman who was below us. Unbeknownst to me, Denise didn't want to reenter the water. The situation was too alien. It was even dangerous. Nonetheless, her Type A personality prevailed and she sloshed back into the stream.

The next matter was the other fisherman. I explained the etiquette of not disturbing the water in casting range of a nearby fisherman, which she found exotic. For Denise, this was a revelation that fly-fishing had rules; it wasn't just a matter of catching fish on a fly. She thought, she said later, that these rules were probably a concoction of a male need to order the world, and also maybe to control territory. For me, a fisherman already in the stream was the equivalent of a red stoplight at an intersection. I might calculate how close I could get without his becoming vocally upset, but I'd never dream of invading the core of the space he was fishing. I told Denise I would fish above and then below the fisherman to our meeting point.

Denise watched me fish, evidently surprised by the intensity of my concentration. Not knowing much about me at that point, she saw a passion that intrigued her. "I liked in you what you obviously loved," was the way she later described her feeling. She decided then, she told me later, that it might be in her interest to find out more about me.

Denise's idea of fishing at that stage was that one had to catch fish. Miraculously, that day she did! A few moments after she'd rejoined me downstream, I saw the tip of her rod bend sharply toward the water. Denise didn't realize what had happened. I did.

I shouted, "You have one . . . lift the rod tip . . . don't pull in hard . . . don't allow slack in the line . . . play the fish. . . let it tire." Despite my instructions, Denise kept cool, the fish remained hooked, and it tired. I took hold of the leader and grabbed in my fist a rather pretty nine-inch brown trout. With a chop of the edge of my hand to the trout's head, I killed it. I praised Denise. We admired the trout briefly, and I proceeded to gut it in the usual manner. Denise was as fascinated by this ritual as my children had been. However, they took it as a given while she, with more perspective on what constitutes normal human behavior, figured this must be a "male thing" with which she hadn't been familiar.

We decided to present the fish as an hors d'oeuvre at a small dinner we were giving in New York. The day of the dinner, I moved the fish from my refrigerator in Connecticut to my briefcase, and then took it by train to the refrigerator of the Swiss Bank Corporation branch in New York where I was on assignment. The next moves were to the refrigerator of the Princeton Club, where I had a squash game after work, and finally to Denise's apartment. I baked it, we garnished it with lemon and parsley, and we set it on a large platter for photographs and display. The guests were gracious enough to act as if the trout were a great delicacy. In any event, for Denise the ceremony at the serving end of the experience was almost as important as seeing my excitement and approbation when she caught it.

As matters turned out, I found in my wife what I'd been seeking in my children—someone with whom to share the joys of fishing, and perhaps, as the years progress and my vision and dexterity decline, to help me tie small flies to thin leaders and maybe even to tell me in what direction the trout lie.

For Denise, fly-fishing was a new aspect of life, entirely different from anything she'd ever experienced. Her family and friends were incredulous at the story that Denise was to be found from time to time not only in the woods but also up to her chest in cold, rushing water. However, photographs drove home the truth. They were amazed. "Must be love," some said.

Prior to our marriage, Denise was registered for wedding presents at The Sportsman's Den, our neighborhood source of fishing tips, rumors about where to go and when, what to use once there, and gossip about other fishermen. Subsequently, homemaking and fishing interests merged but in a manner entirely unanticipated by me. Having been born on Valentine's Day, Denise used hearts as a decorating motif; for me, she chose fish and fishing. Hitherto bare white walls of my apartment were covered with fish prints, and one room carries a paper border of a fisherman casting over and over again. In a cupboard is a set of a dozen Limoges dishes and a platter painted with a variety of fish, which we lugged from a French village where we had bought them for the equivalent of $110. A wedding present of a fish net with frame of polished hardwoods too exquisite to use for fishing hangs from a wall hook beribboned and festooned with a couple of lures. Related objects abound, including a set of aluminum bookends embossed with leaping bass and matching postage stamp dispenser, a birthday present from Denise's mother; a pewter creel paper weight; from an aunt of Denise's catering to what she might have considered to be the peculiar whims of her niece's new husband, a brass sign on small chain stating, "Gone Fishing"; and from Denise's sister, still another sign, this one in the shape of a heart with the wording, "This Marriage Is Interrupted for the Fishing Season." As certain as tomorrow's sunrise, there will be more.

Denise came close to giving up the sport on our first major venture, a day-long trip to a New York State–managed three-thousand-acre preserve with its own lovely stream. What I thought would appeal to her were the setting and the conditions. The stream is narrow but in places surprisingly deep containing, as is common to many such streams in both the eastern and western United States, bright green starwort that undulates in the current and provides nourishment and cover to skuds, leeches, and nymphs, and cover also to trout. Water coming from springs underneath is a constant fifty-four to fifty-six degrees, ideal for year-round insect propagation and trout fattening. Fishing is restricted to barbless, unweighted flies, and the take is limited as well. The stream is full of trout, many of them large, most of them born in a hatchery on the premises. The stream flows through the hatchery, and the fish are healthy and for the most part of good color. Moreover, accustomed to food periodically being dropped down to them, they are usually easy to catch.

Denise's premonition of trouble occurred when we signed up for all three time periods, including the last, from 4 P.M. to sundown. Denise was familiar, albeit not in a friendly way, with cockroaches, silverfish, and other vermin that infest urban American apartment houses, but she was unaccustomed to being immediately accessible to rural varieties of unknown number, shape, and size. Ratcheting up the degree of terror was the prospect of experiencing this wildlife in other than broad daylight. Although outwardly calm, Denise was concerned, to say the least. I assured her that we could leave at any time after 4 P.M., assuming that when dusk came, she'd realize that this was the best fishing time and would want to stay. I failed to anticipate not only the extent of her terror of dark in the woods but also the frustration she would experience before dark ever came.

On the stream, Denise went through what is a common fly-fishing phenomenon. She was hooking flies onto bushes instead of fish, and the flies that she managed to land on water were being ignored by fish dimpling the surface, feeding all around her, and even swimming between her legs. She was in the midst of a prolific, active insect hatch, the dream-come-true of experienced fly-fishers. Such a situation would upset the equanimity of the most patient, veteran angler. The principal difference between Denise and an experienced fly-fisher was that the latter would realize that the trout were not deliberately spiteful, and that with the right analysis of what they were feeding on and the availability in the fly box of a reasonable imitation thereof, the chances of catching one would be reasonably good. Of course, there is always the chance that the natural insect would be too small or unusual to identify, or that the right artificial, or even a close match, would be missing from the fly box.

Needless to say, Denise was ready to go home early. Yet, when dusk came, she saw me fishing. Then dark came, and I was still fishing. I was catching progressively larger fish, none of which had been at all evident earlier. Denise saw that I was showing no inclination whatsoever to stop. What was going through my mind was that Denise would want to share in the abundance of now less-wary, hungry fish that had come out of hiding to hunt down a meal. A slight edge to her voice then warned me otherwise, and that prime fishing notwithstanding, it was time to go.

A year later, we returned. A lot had happened in the interim. Denise had become aware of the *gestalt* common to most experienced fly-fishermen that catching fish isn't necessary to declare a fishing day a success. The process is more important than the results. Most experienced fishermen are reconciled to fishing conditions mirroring life in its imperfections. They look to other factors, even just being out-of-doors, as compensation.

Subsequently, Denise arranged trips for us to two fly-fishing Meccas. One was the San Juan River in northern New Mexico, which she'd learned about during a lunch with a business associate. Neither one of them had known before that the other fly-fished; both were amazed. For Denise, that was serendipity. He'd known her for years as a confirmed-for-life urban dweller, not a person one might even think of as an angler, and before, she'd had no reason even to raise the subject of angling with him. The second trip, a year later, was to the Yellowstone River in southern Montana.

On the San Juan, Denise caught the first fish of the day— a fat, strong rainbow of seventeen inches—on a fly almost too small for the human eye to discern tied to a leader the width of the strand of a spider web. I was so proud that tears came to my eyes. On the Yellowstone, on a particularly bad day, she caught the only trout—another fat rainbow, nineteen inches long—on a fly not much larger than the one she'd used on the San Juan. Unfortunately, I missed the catching of that fish, being upstream out of shouting distance; Denise was sorely disappointed, she said.

For those two trips, I engaged guides. The primary reason was to dissipate the pressure I feared I'd otherwise impose on Denise's fishing methods. A secondary reason was we'd benefit from local knowledge of conditions and techniques, which tend to become increasingly strange the farther one is from one's home waters. On both counts, my judgment proved right. Flies and their presentation are not the same on either river as back East, especially on the San Juan, where twenty-inch-long trout barely moving in deep pockets gently sip tiny emergers and aquatic worms.

Each guide was different. The first was a totally dedicated albeit young man whose task wasn't all that difficult. Although abundant, the variety of aquatic foods on the San Juan was small, making decisions easier. The second guide, Jim Adams, told us that he'd been guiding in Montana for a year and a half. Alarms started clanging about my head, and Denise's, too, it turned out. However, Jim was an expert. He just didn't especially want to talk about himself. Over the course of a couple of days, we learned that he owned a fly-fishing shop in Austin, Texas; that he started fly-fishing as a boy in Tanzania and Kenya, where his parents were serving as Baptist medical missionaries (he as a physician and she a nurse); that he'd fly-fished just about everywhere else in the world; and to Denise's special delight, she being a literary agent, that he was married to a granddaughter of Ernest Hemingway and, with his brother, was starting a bookstore in Uganda, the first to be allowed there since the advent of the dictator Idi Amin. Unlike most guides, who pack for their customers' lunch a loaf of bread, some cold cuts and spreads, and beer and soda, Jim laid out on a linen tablecloth with napkins a repast of hot and cold dishes with sauces he'd prepared the night before and appropriate wine. Denise was enchanted. Jim's was a hard act to follow.

My wish for a spousal fishing partner had crystallized years before I met Denise. While I was Atlantic salmon fishing once in Canada, my attention was caught by a couple on the opposite side of the wide but gentle Miramichee, casting together shoulder by shoulder, with equal expertise, working their way methodically upriver. A heavy mist made the scene ethereal; the realities of their ages, faces, and personalities didn't intrude into the image I was forming. Although the word "romantic" is not part of my vocabulary, what came to mind was a pair of swans, which are said to mate forever, gliding together, gracefully, through life.

The appearance the couple conveyed may not have been the reality. In fact, for all I knew, if one of them had caught a salmon, the other might have become envious. Perhaps one always fished ahead of the other, having first crack at waiting salmon, and the second harbored a long but unspoken resentment about it. We all know that couples react toward each other in different and often strange ways; of course, each couple is unique, and of course, relationships change. Nonetheless, evidence from others indicates that the romantic aspect of my vision of the couple on the Miramichee could have been more real than not.

"We fished together all the time," Joan Wulff said of Lee. "We became each other's favorite companion." Another fisher of renown, Linda Morgens, for thirteen years a national director of Trout Unlimited, a seventy-five thousand–member conservation organization, said of fishing with her husband, Ned, "We're like two pals on the river. It's really wonderful!"

Nonetheless, a fishing relationship is fragile. If it is to survive the emotional dangers it confronts and even grow, it must be nurtured thoughtfully.

Joan and Lee Wulff found that rules obviated some potential stress. "We'd share," Mrs. Wulff said. "For bonefishing [from a flat-bottomed skiff propelled in shallow Caribbean water by a guide with a pole with room on the prow for one caster], we'd each do a half hour, unless one wanted to give time to the other, for example, if a fish was coming to the fly. In a salmon pool [where fishing usually is limited to one person at a time], we'd share the rod. On a trout stream, he'd ask, 'Which area do you want?' "

The Morgenses' modus operandi is similar. Fishing the big Montana rivers from a raft, they even take turns rowing.

In her school, Mrs. Wulff separates couples. Couples tend to have unrealistic emotional expectations of each other, and these can hinder the learning process, she says. One partner, interested in the progress of the other, will look over at the other and say something that's perhaps meant to be helpful but isn't. Each starts thinking of the other; concentration is broken.

Independence is crucial to the couple's maintaining an emotional equilibrium on the water as well, Mrs. Wulff noted. Women must be able to manage for themselves, at least in the basics such as knowing the knots with which to tie a leader to a line and a fly to the leader. "Dependency becomes welfare," Mrs. Wulff says. "It's not good for fishing. The idea is for one not to be dependent upon the other, so the other is not distracted. . . . Fishing time is so precious. You never get enough."

Unlike many women, both Mrs. Wulff and Mrs. Morgens came to their relationships as experienced fly-fishers. In fact, Mrs. Wulff had been fishing for thirty years when she came to know Lee. She began at the age of ten, seeking the attention of her father, for whom fishing, after his family, was his prime love. Ignoring Joan, the father was teaching her younger brothers to cast. While he was at work one day, Joan took his rod to a nearby lake and tried to figure out what to do. In the process, the tip of the three-section rod came apart and flew into the lake. In tears, she confessed to her father. To her surprise, he not only forgave her but encouraged her to continue. Of course, she became more adept at fly-casting than her father and brothers, and just about everyone else in the world.

Mrs. Morgens's upbringing was different. She was the only child of parents who were deep-sea tournament fishers. For them, there was no problem with her being a girl. Her earliest memory is of fishing for sunfish with her father from a dock on a lake in Maine with bobber and bait. With increasing interest and expertise, she moved on to bait fishing for black bass then landlocked salmon, and in due course, fly-fishing for trout and more exotic fish.

Thus, both women were pretty much equals to the men who would become their spouses when they met. Joan had been the co-owner of a dance studio in which she specialized in tap and baton-twirling. "I could have done that until I retired, but I wanted to get into fishing as a profession, which in the fifties was hard." In due course, Joan ended up with Garcia, a fishing equipment manufacturer. About this time, Lee was producing a film for ABC Television on tuna fishing in Newfoundland. His fishing partner was to be Kay Starr, a singer. However, Miss Starr became ill on the filming date, ABC turned to Garcia for help, and the rest is history. Joan and Lee were married a little more than a year later.

One kind of fish Joan didn't know about before her marriage was Atlantic salmon. Lee introduced her to Atlantic salmon fly-fishing. But to learn, she had to adapt to his teaching personality. "He would say, 'Watch me,' " Mrs. Wulff said, "but I had to figure out for myself what I was supposed to be looking for." A major problem for her was the weight of her eight-and-a-half-foot rod. Women, she said, have about half the strength of men. He gave her a six-foot rod of the type he was using then, but casting far with such a short rod was difficult. He had developed an oval, side-arm cast in place of the traditional overhead cast. Evidently, he thought the new cast would be easier to demonstrate than explain. Another example was Lee's preference for the speed of a wet fly in water, fishing for salmon. The line can belly ahead of the fly, behind it, or flow with the current. Again, Mrs. Wulff had to figure out for herself which was the method he thought best.

The Morgenses discovered each other's interest in fishing on their first date. They had agreed to meet at Grand Central Terminal in New York but her train was very late. He went to Abercrombie & Fitch and bought some flies. The train arrived, and seated in a restaurant, he told her how he had occupied his time. She asked to see the flies. When he showed her, to his amazement, she not only named each but described its merits. That wasn't love at first sight, but it came close. Fishing was equally important in their reconciliation after a breakup. He enrolled her in a fly-of-the-month gift program, so every month a new fly would arrive at her doorstep, a monthly reminder of his existence.

Fishing is a good test of character, Mrs. Wulff adds. A person's reaction to adversity, especially cold, miserable weather, clearly demonstrates his or her dignity, humor, consideration, and resolve. "If you can fish with someone, you can live with him," Mrs. Wulff says.

7

FISHING WITH CHILDREN

L
ike most dads bewitched by fishing, I dreamed of having children with whom to share my love of the sport. I would teach them what I know, probably much in the manner of hunter ancestors going back to the beginnings of humanity, albeit, perhaps, with one significant difference. Since survival wasn't at stake, I'd have the luxury of doing so on my own terms, when and how I wanted and with love. I'd be able to savor their success and to participate in their satisfaction while at the same time giving short shrift to their failures. Moreover, once they learned the sport, we'd continue fishing together forever and forever and forever, in eternal familial bliss. Perhaps over time our roles would reverse, and in my dotage, they'd teach me a technique or two they'd discovered, or at least provide help such as tying teeny flies onto near invisible tippets in twilight, always a problem,

or they'd just be company. What a prize! What more could any one person ask from one life!

Of course, it turned out differently. My children's inclinations were not mine.

The first fish my serious, inquisitive son, Peter, caught, I'd caught and released four times. He was five years old, not too young to start, I thought. After all, why postpone heaven? The setting was western Pennsylvania, at a small family summer community not far from the Rolling Rock Club, the Mellon family preserve which includes a hatchery that was probably the first home of Peter's trout, and a designer trout stream, perfected by bulldozers and carpentry. Our own trout stream was too open to predators, especially the human kind, to support a natural population of trout, except at its headwaters, which were little more than a lovely, clear trickle surrounded by thick underbrush.

Peter's trout had chosen as its new home a small, deep hole at a bend in the stream shaded by a large oak tree. Some of the oak's roots extended into the hole, providing further protection for the trout. Any experienced fisherman would recognize this as a great spot. The trout was twelve inches long with the dull color particular to hatchery fish. To assure the success of the first of what I hoped would be a lifetime of fishing ventures with Peter, I wanted to become as familiar as I could with that trout. I caught the trout without much trouble on a barbless hook once one day, twice the next, and a fourth time the following day, always with the same fly when the line straightened out at the same spot in the current. I became concerned that there might be a limit to the fish's credulity. Before the opportunity was lost, I'd better give Peter a go at it.

The time was sunset, perfect for wary as well as ignorant trout, with long shadows changing the light coming to the water. The weather was soft and warm, good for people, too. There couldn't have been a better time.

I walked with Peter, hand in hand, to the tree, replaced the fly on my line with a barbed hook, and attached a worm. I placed Peter just behind the tree, put the rod into one of his hands and the line into the other. I held on to him lightly, and with my hand on his flipped the line, hook, and worm into the current a few feet upstream from the tree. Not to worry.

"Dad, look! I have a fish."

The line lunged under the surface and the rod tip bowed in the same direction. The line zipped around the pool, sketching a V on the surface with the trout occasionally breaking through.

"OK, Peter, you're doing fine," I said, feigning calm. "Just hold on gently. Let it go a little if it wants to. Hold on. You're doing fine."

Somehow, Peter managed, not permitting slack in the line or pulling it too hard. When the struggle slowed, I took the line near the end in one hand, reached into the water with the other, grabbed the trout, and dropped it at my son's feet.

I don't recall Peter's reaction, my attention being consumed by the mechanics of managing his catch and pleasure in our mutual success. We established then a ritual to be followed often in succeeding years. I slit open the belly of the trout, emptied it of its guts, washed it in the stream, and ran a stick through the gill cavity. The skewered trout I gave to Peter to carry home, available for all to see, especially his mother, my first wife.

"Oh, Peter, look what you've caught," she said. "I'm so proud of you!"

The catching of my daughter Ellie's first fish three years later, was less dramatic. Hers was a small sunfish caught on a spinner trolling behind a canoe paddled by her mother and her uncle George.

"By golly, you've got a fish!" George is reputed to have exclaimed. "It's a whopper."

"I'm good, I'm good, I'm good!" Ellie screamed upon seeing the fish, clearly demonstrating the family value system that equated success in fishing with goodness.

Ellie, who was about the same age as Peter had been when he caught his first trout, swung the fish into the boat without having to confront the dark dangers of touching it. After extracting the hook, George returned the fish to its home to grow to a more reasonable size. Nonetheless, both adults said to Ellie, "Yes, indeed, you're good."

The children and I fished often thereafter, but always one on one. Now an adult, Ellie recalls, "This was a time just you and I could be together, without anyone else." There weren't many other occasions when that could occur. Fishing alone with Ellie also established her equality with Peter.

Ellie doesn't remember catching her first trout on a fly rod, in a Montana mountain stream. She was so small I had to lift her and swing her from rock to rock to be in a position to drift the fly downstream into likely eddies and holes. She remembers more recent occasions.

"You bought me those big hip boots," she recalled. "They were enormous. But what I liked was that you said, 'Sometimes you can feel the fish bumping into your legs,' and I imagined that. Thinking I was right among the fish, instead of up on a bank, I was more involved. That was really cool. We walked in the current side by side, and you'd move my hand holding the rod to let the worm float down into a certain spot in the pool, and sometimes a trout would be right there!"

Ellie also recalls a trip in which she caught a fish and I didn't. "Catching that trout made it worthwhile. We stayed forever, and nothing happened, but then it all worked out. I was proud, especially knowing I'd done something you hadn't that you're good at."

Peter recalls almost every fishing venture we took together after the age of eight, including a bass he caught on a farm pond that was so heavy his arm ached carrying it back to the house to show to his mother. He recalls striking bats by mistake with his rod tip while fishing with me under a full moon, and almost catching a barracuda on light tackle in the intercoastal waterway in Florida.

"Do you remember, Dad?" he once asked. "We were standing on this drawbridge, way up. A little fish took my bait, and along came this huge green barracuda out of nowhere. He chomped that fish. He was on the line a minute. What would we have done? I guess you'd have to climb down and grab him."

Peter had one experience alone which excited my imagination more than his, as it turned out. "I was standing on my sail board in the middle of Long Island Sound, and I saw the water frothing in front of me. The wind blew the boat right into it. It was blues. I could feel them banging the centerboard. They even knocked the board back and forth."

Peter was in the midst of a bluefish blitz. The blues were attacking a school of bunker, a kind of herring about a foot long, killing as many as they could as fast as they could, snapping them into two or three chunks and then sweeping around to swallow the pieces. Frightened, Peter lowered the sail so as to slow down and have better balance. He'd been around the Sound long enough to know that if he fell in, he could loose some chunks of himself as well; in a feeding frenzy, blues tend to sink their teeth into anything that moves. In fifteen seconds, it was over. The bunker had moved off, with the blues in pursuit.

I imagined myself joining him, albeit in a sturdier vessel, with rod and reel, preying on the preying bluefish. "I just wanted to get out of there," Peter said. That was the first sign that my dream would not turn out as I had anticipated.

Especially fascinating to both children early on, before they were old enough to take a boat out alone, was gutting the fish we decided to keep. This event took on the characteristics of a ritual, autonomous to the catching of the fish, which I performed under the children's watchful gaze. The maneuvering of knife and fingers inside the fish were precise and always the same. We might have been appeasing the Fish Spirit for removing one of its creatures from life.

"You used to open the stomach to see what was inside," Ellie said. "That was fun. There was all this blood and really gross stuff, but you'd explain that it was important to see what the fish had been eating. It almost became a game—'Oh, let's see what the fish ate.'"

What we found more often than not was small and dark remnants of aquatic insects, indistinguishable from anything they knew, although sometimes we'd distinguish crayfish and beetles. I'd say that the fly we were using or about to use matched what the trout had eaten. However, I'd have to do a bit of guessing, often helped by knowing aforehand which aquatic insects were supposed to be there at that time. The presence of pebbles and hemlock needles in the stomachs of hatchery trout accustomed to food pellets dropped on the surface did not detract from the interest of our investigation.

There was a final moment to the cleaning ritual. "At the end, you'd run the end of your thumb along the inside to take out the goop that was left," Ellie said. "That was a kind of catharsis. Before, I'd feel guilt that we'd killed the fish. Then, after it was cleaned, I could say, 'OK, we're going to eat it.' It's what made the fish edible."

The ritual would be concluded by my throwing the guts into the bushes for any nearby wildlife, thereby extending the life cycle. (Once, just inches from my hand, a red fox poked its head out of a tangle of bushes. We stared at each other, eyeball to eyeball, for a couple of seconds. Then the fox brazenly grabbed the pile of intestines that I'd dropped and disappeared back into the underbrush. The event took less than a minute.)

Neither child ever removed a fish from a hook. "You seemed to like it," Ellie said. She was right, of course. They knew that what counted for me was their catching the fish. They were concerned about my disappointment if they tangled their lines in trees, even though they saw me do this myself, and even though when they did it, I invariably untangled the mess without remonstrance either stated or felt.

Eventually, as the children grew into their teens, other aspects of life became more critical than catching fish to please their dad. They lost interest after an hour or so of fishing, even when they were catching fish, and felt trapped if they knew that more fishing was to be done. Later Ellie was able to say, "Well, I felt a little guilty." Nonetheless, they were not so constrained that when invited to still another fishing venture, they could say, "No thanks, Dad," albeit knowing that this made me sad.

This change in letting me know how they felt occurred gradually, and they handled it with tact. I could do nothing but accept the situation, with disappointment, to be sure, but also with the understanding that this was the way it was to be. The disappointment was tempered by knowing I had actually experienced the dream for several years. The memory is with me now, and always will be. In that sense what I had I still have, and I'm grateful for it.

Different fishing traditions are created in other families.

"My father fished with us when we were little, but he never tried to cram it down our throats," Jeffrey Boyd says. "We started when we were really little, my brother, Gary, and me. He'd take us to piers and we'd sit there catching baby blues with bait. We just did it. Everyone liked the outdoors. It was part of our life." Then there was a period of fishing abstinence.

Scudder Boyd, Jeffrey's father, says, "I fished all my life, and my father fished before me, but then my wife and I suddenly had five kids, and life became too busy. We stopped fishing. But when Jeff was in law school at Cornell, he told us that there were some good trout streams nearby. I found some old equipment and bought some cheap Japanese flies, and went up. We talked to a ranger who directed us to a certain bridge over a certain pool. We caught trout after trout. We've been fishing together, Jeff, Gary, and me, ever since."

Jeff, with whom I find myself occasionally prospecting for striped bass, shoulder to shoulder in Long Island Sound at high tides at sunset or sunrise and sometimes under the moon at night, added, "That was when a lot of things were happening in my father's life that gave him time to spend fishing with us."

Jeff says the experience didn't especially bring him and Scudder any closer—they were always close—but fishing allows them to spend more time with each other. Now, Jeff is teaching his son, age eight, to fish. "I'll expose him to it," Jeff says. "If he likes it, in twenty years maybe he'll thank me."

Donald Kiefer's twin boys needed no encouragement to begin fishing. At age four, they strung a pair of their mother's pantyhose over a bent clothes hanger, thus fashioning a net with which they trapped gold fish that had been dumped into the town pond. While their mother noted the absence of the pantyhose, Donald recognized the call to fishing. He put together some equipment and took them to the same sort of piers where the Boyd brothers fished.

"They'd sit and fish happily all day long," Donald said. "We could leave them with no fear they'd become bored or wander off. It's one of the few activities that absorbed their attention for more than a few minutes." When the boys were eight and in the Florida Keys on vacation, they took up fly-fishing. They're avid fly-fishers now.

"It's one more lovely common thread we have together," Donald says. "We're companions, not just father and sons."

The boys echo their father. Jared finds that fishing with his father permits an intimacy that at best would be difficult in other circumstances. "It's a place to talk to my dad alone," he says. "Like my grades. He won't get mad up there because he's having such a good time. He'll say, 'Oh, we'll talk about that later.' And then he'll forget. He's really into fishing." Taylor adds, "It's fun just being with him. It doesn't matter if we don't catch fish. We're with our dad."

8

EARLY FLY-FISHING

Records of what might be sport fishing, at least fishing with rods and lines, go back to the beginnings of history in China and Egypt. Ernest Schweibert in his book *Trout* writes of the use of silk fishing lines on thornwood rods four thousand years ago during the Chinese Bronze Age, when metal hooks probably were fashioned for the first time. A millennium later, the Chinese sage Chiang Tzu-Ya wrote of fishing being both contemplative and morally edifying, anticipating medieval European thinking. Confucius, also an angler, urged the use of rods instead of less sporty nets. Tapered cane rods and gut leaders also came into use then, long before they did in Europe.

There is mention, Schweibert writes, of what might have been an artificial fly. While trout, grayling, and salmon lived in the north-flowing rivers of Mongolia and Manchuria, the

Chinese were principally interested in carp, which rarely eat insects, an impediment to the development of fly-fishing. (Grayling are a cold-water fish related to trout but even more sensitive to pollution. In the United States, they survive only in portions of Montana and Alaska.)

In Egypt, tomb murals depict people fishing the Nile with rods and lines as well as nets. Evidently, these were ordinary folk as well as nobility. Plutarch described in his *Life of Antonius* Cleopatra's pleasure in fishing:

> She hath used to take delight, with her fair hand
> To angle happily in the Nile, where its glad fishes
> As though they saw who 'twas sought to deceive them
> Contended eagerly to be taken.

Cleopatra and Antony, a brilliant military strategist with a troublesome ego, competed to see who could catch the most fish. Antony was supposed to have had soldiers swim under the royal barge and attach live fish to his hook. Cleopatra, no dummy, figured this out, and had one of her own divers attach a dead fish to his line. Antony fought the fish with fake heroics, to be ridiculed by the young queen when he hauled it on board.

Shakespeare picks up the story in *Antony and Cleopatra:*

> CLEOPATRA. Give me mine angle; we'll to the river: there—
> My music playing far off—I will betray
> Twany-finn'd fishes; my bended hook shall pierce
> Their slimy jaws; and as I draw them up,
> I'll think them every one an Antony,
> And say, "Ah, ha!" you're caught.

> CHARMIAN. 'Twas merry when
> You wager'd on your angling; when your diver
> Did hang a salt-fish on his hook, which he
> With fervency drew up.

CLEOPATRA. That time—O times!—
I laugh'd him out of patience; and that night
I laugh'd him into patience; and next morn,
ere the ninth hour, I drunk him to his bed.

The first published mention of an artificial fly might have occurred as early as the first century. A Roman poet, Marcus Valarius Martialis, some of whose verse is so salacious he has been little published in English, wrote of fish rising and being killed by "fraudful flies" *(scarum musca).* However, the fish he described is a salt-water breed that feeds generally on vegetation, not insects; in one way or another, Martialis seems to have been confused.

Two centuries later, Claudius Aelianus, a Roman essayist, described fly-fishing in a book called *On the Characteristics of Animals,* a miscellany of facts, real and supposed, about the animal kingdom of the known world. Aelianus never left Italy. He relied extensively on ancient and contemporary Greek writers, but for some reason, probably snobbery, not his fellow Romans. His motivation was less the furtherance of science than propounding the tenets of Stoicism. While acknowledging his belief in divine providence, Aelianus contrasted the follies and selfishness of mankind, a target of the Stoics, with the instinctual virtues of the animal world. At that time, hardly anyone in the upper classes gave Christianity any serious thought.
Aelianus wrote:

I have learned about the Macedonian method of fishing, and it is this: . . . These speckled fish feed on insects . . . which flutter over the river . . . When the fish observe a fly on the surface, they swim up stealthily, . . . open their mouths gently and seize the flies . . .
Although the fisherfolk understand this, they cannot use these insects as bait for the fish; for when they are

touched, they lose their natural coloring, their wings wither, and they become unfit for deceiving fish . . .

But fishermen have planned an artful trap. . . . They wrap scarlet wool about their hooks, and wind into the wool two wax-colored feathers that grow under a cock's wattles.

Their rods are about six feet, with a line of similar length. With these, they lower the fly, and the fish, attracted by the colors and thinking of a meal, take it . . . and are caught.

Aelianus called this river the Astraeum. Attempts to identify the river in current as well as ancient gazettes will be futile. According to A. F. Scholfield, who in 1957 translated Aelianus's work *On the Characteristics of Animals* from the original Greek, the river really was the Axius. In Macedonia, it's known now as the Vardar; Prof. Kiril Apostolski in Skopje, Macedonia, confirms that the upper reaches of the river still contain trout.

All that's changed, seventeen hundred years later, is the use of reels to store and then release line for fish to carry until they tire. In those days, the suppleness of the rod was all there was to play a large fish.

Most fascinating of all is Juliana Berners, a noble prioress of a Benedictine nunnery near the Norman cathedral of St. Albans in England in the early fifteenth century. At the end of the century, the Abbey of St. Albans published the *Treatyse of Fysshynge wyth an Angle.* One earlier incomplete handwritten copy is under lock and key at the Beinecke Library at Yale University; others probably were lost or destroyed when Henry VIII encouraged the confiscation of Catholic Church property including the monastical libraries. Little is known about Dame Juliana, other than the fact that she was the daughter of a knight and the sister of a lord and delighted in fishing.

The only mention in the treatise of God and prayer is at

the end, and there is but one scriptural reference. It's a comment by Solomon which Dame Juliana elaborates upon, as translated from the Middle English in which she wrote: "The pleasure and sport of angling is a means and an end to induce a man to become glad of spirit, which . . . renders lifelong flourishing." Dame Juliana was conscious of what today we call mental health. She seems to have seen angling an aid to a sound outlook on life for others as well as herself, and also, for herself, perhaps a respite from the rigors of managing the nunnery.

In addition to providing homes for the truly devoted who, because of their sex, were denied other official positions within the church, nunneries were outlets for educated women who wanted to do something with their lives other than be courtiers or manage households. They were also refuges for ladies who had fallen on hard times, and places where the wealthy were able to house difficult daughters. The prioress had heavy personnel as well as other management responsibilities, with probably only nominal help from the male church hierarchy. Fishing must have been an outlet for the probable frustrations of Dame Juliana's position and also a contributor to her evidently happy disposition. The importance of the sport for her is indicated by the enormous time and close attention she devoted to it.

Besides its prescriptions for healthy living, Dame Juliana's treatise provides a compendium of medieval angling techniques. Fly-fishing was, from A to Z, a do-it-yourself pastime. Dame Juliana advises what wood to select for each of the recommended three sections of the rod, and how to season and heat treat it; how to dye horsehair and weave it into lines for different fish; where to attach lines to rods; how to forge and then temper barbed hooks from steel needles used for embroidering, tailoring, or shoemaking, depending upon how much strength was wanted; how to snell lines under silk windings to the eyeless hooks; how to select, propagate, and care for bait; a recipe of sheep's tallow and cake for feeding maggots to make them fatter and a dip to render worms more appetizing to fish consisting of blood from a sheep's heart mixed in flour and honey; and most especially, for the sixth of six ways to fish, what flies to tie and how, and also when to use each, from March through August.

Although Dame Juliana doesn't say so, probably because she didn't think it was necessary, she is likely as well to have skinned the birds and beasts from which she obtained fly-tying materials. She prefaced the fly section, in the original English, thus:

> Twelve flyes wyth whyche ye shall angle to ye trought and graylynge, and dubbe lyke as ye shall now here me tell.

Evidence indicates that Dame Juliana's formulas for the twelve flies had been around a long time. She makes no claim to having invented them, but one hundred and fifty years later, Izaak Walton lifted them for inclusion in *The Compleat Angler*. Most are still recognizable, while others were either generic or peculiar to the fly hatches of the rivers around St. Albans. Basic fly-fishing hasn't changed much since the *Treatyse* was written.

Earthly pleasures, including angling, were morally suspect in Dame Juliana's time. Thus, to avoid questions of propriety, Dame Juliana recommended use of a rod with a hollow bored in the butt section to accommodate the other sections of the rod, thereby disguising the whole as a walking stick. Then, Dame Juliana wrote, ". . . no man will know the errand on which you are going."

Dame Juliana described fishing etiquette in a formula that still applies today. She advised refraining from taking fish from another's weir, especially if it's in private water, adding that if readers pay sufficient attention to the instructions in the treatise, they'll catch enough so that stealing won't be necessary. She suggested shutting gates; taking care not to break any hedges; and keeping only those fish that are to be eaten.

Readers wouldn't realize from the tone of the *Treatyse* and

The Compleat Angler the social and political turbulence of their times. Dame Juliana may have been composing her treatise at the time the fourteen-year-old peasant Joan of Arc led the French uprising against the English, subsequently to be captured, tried as a heretic, and burned alive. It was an era of fear, superstition, and terror. England suffered from a brutal, avaricious aristocracy, corruption in the royal court, famines in the countryside, and periodic revolts by the overwrought population. Izaak Walton, a century and a half later, lived and wrote during the Puritan rebellion against an oppressive, shortsighted British monarchy. Oliver Cromwell's cavalry rode into battle to slaughter their Anglican, Catholic, and Presbyterian foes while singing hymns. Walton, a Royalist, was on the opposing side. No hint of these temporal problems intrudes in either work; the wonders and workings of God's world manifested through angling transcend all.

Walton, of Staffordshire yeoman background, made a fortune in ironworks. At the age of fifty he retired to the country, where for the next forty years he fished, contemplated life, and wrote. *The Compleat Angler,* first published in 1653 when Walton was sixty, saw five editions in his lifetime and is said by some to be the most published book in English next to the Bible. As in real life, for every one part of actual fishing in the book, there are one hundred of talk about fishing.

Little information in *The Compleat Angler* was new; fishing, especially fly-fishing, hadn't changed much since Dame Juliana's time. Besides, Walton was basically a bait fisherman. Even the format of the book, a discussion between hunter, falconer, and fisherman on the merits of each man's favorite recreation, had been done before. Walton's contribution was to describe angling, simply, cheerfully, and effectively, as a celebration of life and even God.

"God never did make a more calm, quiet, innocent recreation than Angling," he wrote.

Views on temporal recreation had become, if anything,

stricter in Walton's time, when the Puritans (whose aim was to "purify" the Anglican Church) dominated political as well as religious practice, but even the clergy applauded the book. Of course, their attention was directed to Walton's emphasis on the spiritual aspects of fishing rather than his fishing instruction. The book is liberally bestowed with references to the Scriptures and also Greek, Latin, and contemporary sages. The early prophets Moses and Amos, he tells us with some hyperbole, were anglers, not just fishermen. In the rewriting of successive editions, Walton became increasingly preachy. Nonetheless, the book remains one of the great idylls of a sport.

In technical terms, Walton's expertise was bait fishing. One can see his delight in the sport just by the attention he gives to describing proper selection and care of live bait. In fact, to this day, his information on this subject is unsurpassed. Walton recommends, by way of example, the Brandling worm, which one finds under rotting cow or hog dung but not horse dung, which is too warm and dry. If the worms become listless or thin, he suggests dropping a little milk or cream or even a beaten egg on the moss upon which they're supposed to rest. The moss should be fresh (he tells us what "fresh" is), and some kinds of moss are preferable to others. If ground worms are hard to come by in dry midsummer, he advises squeezing walnut leaves into water and then pouring the water onto the ground; the acidity of the mix will induce the worms to the surface overnight. Besides worms, Walton provides us a lot of information on the use of minnows, frogs, and even cheese balls, which he recommends blending with butter and saffron for color.

When Walton comes to describe fly-fishing, his enthusiasm, and as a result his prose, flagged. Evidently to remedy this situation, he took on a collaborator, Charles Cotton, who added a second and now integral part to *The Compleat Angler,* beginning with the fifth edition. Cotton, a local squire and minor poet, was a more accomplished fly-fisher than Walton, albeit not as good a writer, his prose being somewhat self-conscious.

Nonetheless, the collaboration was good for both. Cotton, thirty-seven years younger than Walton, doesn't cease to pay homage in his part of the book to "the Master" and "Father Walton." The two, in the formal style of the time, became fast friends.

Fly-fishing in the midseventeenth century consisted of what was known as dabbing. Crawling or knee-walking, dressed in what we imagine the American Pilgrims wore on the first Thanksgiving, the angler crept up to a likely spot along a bank, perhaps where he knew there was an overhang or cut under the bank that would provide a safe lie for trout. Without showing himself, the angler would poke a rod twice the length of today's rods over the water and drop the bait or fly into the current, allowing a minimum of line to touch the surface. Sometimes, the angler would watch whatever he placed at the end of his line, but more often he would listen for a strike.

Because there were no reels, except for some awkward wooden spools used on salmon rods, the trout angler's line was attached near the tip of the rod, with the maximum line length he could handle being usually no more than twelve feet. In those days fishermen were so few that trout could live to become quite large. Twenty inches was not uncommon, and one of Walton's catches, traced on a board that was hung at a nearby tavern, was said to be close to three feet. Upon hooking a trout too large for his equipment and skill, Walton would throw his whole rig into the water and allow the fish to drag the mess about until it tired. Then he would retrieve the rig and, he hoped, the fish. Cotton scolded Walton, "Master" or not, for this want of sportsmanship.

Although these people and their methods may seem primitive, fishing then was not unsophisticated. Rods were made for sale in London, anglers spent a lot of time considering their sport, and they knew to a surprising degree just what they were doing. Witness Cotton's instruction for garnering material for the dubbing, or body, of the Blue Dun.

Take a small tooth comb, and with it comb the neck of a black greyhound, and the down that sticks to the teeth will be the finest blue you ever saw.

Natural colors were preferable to dyes. Other materials Cotton recommends for specific flies include the whirl of an ostrich feather and the black spot of a hog's ear. Similar natural materials are used now. With the discovery of additional materials, reexamination of aquatic insects, and development of tying skills, Cotton increased the number of artificial flies from Berners's and Walton's basic twelve to fifty-five.

Cotton advised fishing far and fine, as an instructor might today. He lengthened the amount of line he could handle so his flies could reach as far as thirty-five feet. By fine, he meant light line near the fly. Dame Juliana advocated lines tapering down to twelve strands of horsehair for trout. Walton said three at least. Cotton reduced the number to two, which could hold a feisty twenty-inch trout only with skill.

THEODORE GORDON

The inquiry into catching trout on an artificial fly described by Dame Juliana extends to a turn-of-the-century American angler, Theodore Gordon. Perhaps the first person to devote his life to angling, Gordon plays a major albeit controversial role in American fly-fishing history.

He also played a role in my understanding of the sport. Having read about him, I began a late-life quest to learn more, which led me, among other places, to the vault in which he and his mother and a cousin are interred in a seldom-visited grassy half-acre nineteenth-century graveyard surrounded by two- and three-story tenements in lower Manhattan.

John McDonald, in *The Complete Fly Fisherman: The Notes and Letters of Theodore Gordon,* called him "perhaps the only man ever to express with his whole life the ideal of the anglers' brotherhood." Paul Schullery, while recognizing Gordon's importance in contemporary fly-fishing, expressed another view in *American Fly Fishing:*

> He is unrivaled in his importance as a symbol, and he is rarely matched in his qualities as a writer and angling thinker. But he has been unfairly jerked from his context by our half-century binge of admiration.

The invention in England of the dry fly around the turn of the century was a pivotal moment in fly-fishing. Heretofore, wet flies, i.e., those designed to sink, were used. With dry fly-fishing came fishing upstream, instead of down, which required a different, more difficult technique. But the dry fly patterns first developed in England imitated English insects, some of which don't exist in the United States. Gordon was one of the first to imitate American insects and also to adapt fly construction to faster American water.

The Quill Gordon, which he invented, is still used. Of the real fly, the scientific name of which is *Epeorus pleuralis Banks,* Art Flick exclaimed in his well-known *Streamside Guide,* "How I welcome the day this fly makes its first appearance each season, for it means that at long last the dry fly season has arrived."

Sport fishing in this country, McDonald wrote, was unknown before 1830. "Fish was food." But when Gordon was a boy in the eighteen-sixties, fly-fishing took off. Major changes were wrought: logging and mining destroyed vast habitats; fishing waters, once open to all, were privatized by anglers and angling clubs; the native eastern brook trout was nearly eliminated by overfishing and the hardier, warier, larger-growing German brown trout was introduced.

Gordon is seen by some as an angler's Henry David Thoreau. Their time on earth overlapped by only eight years (Gordon was born in 1854 and Thoreau died in 1862) but the styles in which they conducted their lives were similar. Both lived as writers close to nature and as partial recluses for long periods, although in Gordon's case, the choice, at least initially, may not have been his first.

Born in Pittsburgh to a family in comfortable circumstances, tragedy occurred early and followed Gordon thereafter. Gordon's father died when he was young, and afterward his mother moved from place to place, doing her best to make his life easy. As a young man, he worked intermittently in brokerage offices, and began increasingly lengthy fishing trips in the Catskills. In due course, his mother's fortunes failed as did her health. His health failed as well, since he'd been born with respiratory problems. He moved to the Catskills, where he lived somewhat hand-to-mouth for the remainder of his life. He became a professional fly tier, wrote for British and American fishing journals, and spent a lot of time observing the activities of fish and insects on his beloved Beaverkill and Neversink rivers.

Consider the following excerpts from Gordon's writings gathered in *The Complete Fly Fisherman:*

Anglers are patient, hopeful people. All the fatigues and misfortunes of the pursuit are forgotten, or form subjects for jokes or amusing reminiscences. We remember our first trout and nearly all of our big fish until the last day of our lives.

I am sorry to say that free water is decreasing rapidly. It will soon be impossible to get a day's sport within a hundred miles of our large cities without being a member of a club or paying for the privilege in some way. I would not care to fish only in a well-stocked preserve, and as for catching trout that I had bred and raised, I fear that such sport would possess few attractions for me.

The big hare that turns white in winter sits out in all weathers, but seems to retire to the evergreen swamps during the day. This fellow can cover ground like a racehorse, when scared or pursued, and hops about four feet when taking things slow.

My fingers itch to open any old fly-book I see. [Fly-book means pouch, usually leather with the fur inside, for holding flies.]

If I thought that trout were colour-blind, or nearly so, I am afraid that I would lose at least one-half the delight I have in fly fishing. While the snow-water was in the river and there was not a fly hatching last week, I could not take a trout until I tied up a thing intended to resemble a large larva or nymph, with a red tag. With that, in a few hours in two afternoons, I killed thirteen trout from 2 1/2 lb. down. None of the native fly-fishers would go out, as they said it was useless; the trout would not rise.

I believe that fly fishing has a good influence on character. We make many lasting friendships through our love of it, and receive many benefits and much help through the kindly sentiments which it inspires. When I was a small, rather weakly lad, middle-aged and elderly men inconvenienced themselves greatly to gratify my love of sport. One of them used to carry me from one side to the other of a river which was too deep for me to wade with my short legs. An enthusiastic small boy is not always the most desirable companion on a fishing trip.

9

FISHING ABROAD

The business end of a long, ugly, Serbian-made semi-automatic rifle was aimed at my chest, the face of a frightened green-clad teenager behind it. His nervousness made me nervous. I froze. My first thought was: "Don't alarm this guy any more than he already is." My next was more reflective: "You just can't tell what will happen when you go fishing."

I had wandered into a Yugoslav army camp. I'd often been driven by the camp, which alongside the road was bordered by a fence complete with bored sentries. Below the camp, in a ravine, was the Sava Bohinka, the finest river I'd ever seen, usually deep but with a translucent green quality. It was the home of large trout and grayling. I had left the river after a day's fishing, clambered up the mountain slope, and unaware of just where I was, walked into the camp from the rear, where there were no barriers.

Quickly, I was surrounded by other soldiers, speaking to each other in Slovenian, a language spoken by as many people who live in Colorado. I didn't think I looked like much of a threat. I was clad in chest waders which inhibit movement of most any kind, and there wasn't much damage I could do with the slender fly rod I continued to hold. However, who knew what my fishing vest concealed. In due course, an English-speaking corporal arrived, and I was marched to a command post. Inside, a lieutenant sat behind an empty desk. In universal military style, he established his authority by never giving me a glance. He asked questions of the corporal, who asked questions of me. I established my *bone fides* as an American angler, was escorted to the front gate, and released.

If my primary language had been Russian, I thought, I might not have arrived on the other side of that gate for a long time. Although the Soviet Union and Yugoslavia both were Communist, the culture of the Slovenians has been shaped more by the Austro-Hungarian Empire than the Soviet empire.

I came to Slovenia a couple of times a year for two reasons. One was to check on the progress of a steel mill which had purchased several million dollars' worth of U.S. equipment with loans I had arranged. The second was to fish.

In the early stages of negotiating the loan, the treasurer of the mill had come to Pittsburgh, bringing along financial projections, engineering plans, and color photographs of the site where a new cold rolling mill was to be placed. In the background were majestic, snow-covered mountains. "Looks like Colorado," I remarked. "Any trout there?" "Sure," he replied. "When you come, we'll fix you up." Right then, a surge of adrenaline poked up my heart rate.

When the time finally arrived, I wasn't disappointed. Not only was the fishing great, but so was what accompanied it. That first morning, and many mornings to follow, I was picked up at the lovely lakeside hotel that had been a spa for wealthy Europeans at the turn of the century. The mode of transportation to the river was a large, polished black Mercedes with driver. In charge of the expedition was the English-speaking fly-fishing manager of the hot rolling mill. He and I would fish until two in the afternoon when the driver, transformed into maitre d', spread a white linen tablecloth on the ground and set out a lunch of bread, cheese, cold cuts, wine, and plum brandy called *slivovitz,* all produced in the neighborhood.

This angler's heaven-on-earth continued several years until the treasurer retired. At lunch in the officers' dining hall of the mill on a Friday during my next visit, I waited for his successor to ask when I'd like to be picked up the next morning to fish. Nothing happened, except an anxiety attack; my pulse raced; I felt faint. I was being abandoned to my own devices. That night, musings on the withdrawal of the security, comfort, and convenience of the prior arrangements tossing around my head, I slept hardly at all. But by the next morning, I had a plan.

The attendant at the front desk wrote for me the name of the village closest to the spot on the river where I wanted to be. I purchased a day's license and, gear in hand, set out to the bus stop. For the equivalent of four cents, I was driven to my destination up the valley, not in the style to which I'd become accustomed but without mishap. I scrambled down the mountainside and fished, alone but pleased to bits at my newfound independence. Midafternoon, I clambered back up the mountainside; trudged, waders over a shoulder, to a nearby café; enjoyed a meal of grilled meat and vegetables, washed down by *slivovitz;* called a taxi; and rode back, tired and even more satisfied, to the hotel. That was my new fishing pattern, varied occasionally by a trip with a hotel employee who fly-fished and owned a run-down Polish-made Fiat, which he repaired once with some string he found lying on the road.

This being the northern, Roman Catholic, tidy and orderly end of the country, licenses, obtained by the day for a specific area of the river, were checked. Custom had it that after the warden found all in order, one shared a swallow of one's *slivovitz* with him. Once, however, the warden found me out of order, for reasons I couldn't understand. He shouted at me, red-in-the-face, in Slovenian, and tore a streamer off my leader. Hearing the commotion, a companion along with me that day rushed downriver to translate. "He's not at all happy," my companion remarked, needlessly. "He says you weren't using a dry fly. Your license specifies dry flies only." My companion explained something to him. I apologized. Then, as an experiment, I showed the warden my box of small wet flies. *"Da! Da!"* He nodded vigorously, smiling for the first time. Seems that the streamer which had been too small to hold a spectacularly large fish a few moments prior to my arrest was too large to comply with his definition of a dry fly. In any event, he forgave me.

I fished in other areas of Yugoslavia, including what is now the country of Macedonia to the south. What a difference! The hospitality was even grander, but rules? People believed they existed, but no one had any idea of just what they were, to say nothing of enforcing them. Try as I might, I couldn't even find an official to sell me a fishing license. The other side of the coin was that the fish were smaller and less abundant than in Slovenia.

One particularly spectacular trip was arranged by the gracious, effective chief executive officer of a metal goods manufacturing company to which my bank had lent money for the purchase of a Pennsylvania-made extrusion press. The trip commenced with a dinner for ten at a fine restaurant that had been converted from a Dervish monastery (now in the process of reclamation by the monks, to the consternation of local Orthodox Catholic government officials). From there, we drove in a caravan of Mercedes limousines to the top of a mountain with a ski lift, at which point we switched to Soviet army jeeps, and proceeded over rutted, dirt roads deep into the mountain range. We passed ragged, barefoot children tending sheep with large dogs, spike collars around their necks for protection from wolves. The dogs rushed the jeeps, jaws agape, howling, with the children howling after them in a language my host didn't understand. It was Albanian, I figured out later, the language of my paternal forebears who had settled in this area thousands of years before the arrival of the Slavs and probably even before the Helenes came to what is now Greece. A few thousand bumps and jolts later, we arrived at our destination, a hunting lodge in a high clearing surrounded by dark forest. Dinner was prepared by a company cook and assistant over a wood fire but served on linen tablecloths; it included a variety of grilled meats, peppers, potatoes, salads, and of course fine local red and white wines and *slivovitz.*

I was awakened before dawn by the designated guide, stumbled outside trying not to waken the others, splashed frigid water from a bucket on my face, and guide ahead of me, clambered down the mountain, fly rod in hand, to the gurgling of a small stream. The guide and I began to fish. Partly because he was using a spinning rod, an apparent cultural gap, and because we didn't speak the same language, a real cultural gap, I moved ahead of him. I caught occasional small brown trout, none of which I thought large enough to keep. Eventually, we met. With a wide grin, he displayed a bucket filled with these small trout. For him to return to the lodge without trout would have been a humiliation. Besides, small trout are as good to eat as any other. The reason the trout were small and also not numerous, however, was that they were killed as fast as they could be caught. I learned later that children, probably also Albanians from villages far below, trudged up the mountain, equipped with a few feet of monofilament line and heavy weights to take baited hooks to hungry trout at the pool bottoms. Not exactly a sporting way to fish, but food rather than sport probably was what was on their minds.

Fishing abroad with a fly rod tends to be similar to that in the United States although the settings and customs, as I found, can be different, and in some cases, the fish are as well.

NORWAY

Of the varieties of salmon, Atlantic is the best. Unlike the others, Atlantic salmon don't necessarily die after they spawn.

As a result, they can live longer, become smarter, and grow larger than most other salmon. Also, fly-fishing for Atlantic salmon, formerly the sport of European nobility (because they owned the rivers), is steeped in tradition. Atlantic salmon can be found in lots of places where cold-water rivers open to the Atlantic. Now that Russia is accessible to Westerners, Atlantic salmon fishing trips are being organized to Siberia, where the locals have learned fast how to exploit a penchant of some anglers for the new and exotic. Atlantic salmon have always been there, but few if any anglers have fished for them until recently. Before Siberia, Iceland was the place to go; it's now expensive. Efforts are under way to reintroduce the Atlantic salmon to Connecticut, where in Colonial times they swam up virtually every river and stream connected to salt water. But of all these places, Norway and Scotland are the favorites among fly-fishing traditionalists. The scenery in both is spectacular, although in different ways, but Norway isn't plagued by biting insects in the summer the way Scotland and other northern countries are.

Pat Hemingway, retired forestry officer in East Africa for the Food and Agricultural Organization of the United Nations, outfitter to big-game hunters, and son of the author of the same name, says, "If I ever wanted to be a citizen of a country other than the United States, I'd pick Norway. It's beautiful, a very pleasant place." In Norway, his choice for salmon fishing is the River A (pronounced "Oh").

"There's a high plateau that plunges into a sheltered fjord," Mr. Hemingway says. "The climate is marine, fresh and cool with the smell of salt air, and there are lots of small, bright wildflowers. It doesn't get dark except for a couple of hours, which leaves lots of fishing time. We stay at a very plain lodge, with three guest rooms like monk cells, and a large dining and social room overlooking the river. To fish, we just walk fifty yards down to the first pool. There's a guide for every two rods, a Norwegian, a Swede, and a Finn. The river is small, like the West Gallatin [in Montana]. The fish are a good size, ten to twenty-five pounds, and utterly bright. [Bright means the salmon have come into the river recently, at the peak of their strength. Their color darkens after they've been in the river awhile.] They're strong, so you have to be careful to keep them in the pool where you've hooked them. Otherwise, they're gone. It's quite wonderful."

Because the salmon don't generally feed in the rivers, fishing for them is different from fishing for trout, when one can apply entomological and other knowledge and at least expect success. The taking of salmon on a fly is entirely unpredictable. Mr. Hemingway comments, "People fool themselves into thinking it's a special fly or technique. It's luck." Less dogmatic or romantic salmon anglers would agree.

Having been a guide himself, Mr. Hemingway is especially sensitive to quality of service on fishing trips. "It's one of the things I feel about very strongly," he says. "I've fished all over North America, and I've yet to find it. Guides don't know how to make people comfortable. They don't want to learn; they think it's beneath them." However, in Norway, service is a tradition. "The lodge owner and his wife rent the area from local farmers. He runs a jewelry shop at other times. This is a summer project. She's an attractive young blonde, and a master cook. A typical meal consists of salmon caught by one of the guests in a bed of aspic surrounded by artichoke hearts with other locally grown vegetables, flan for dessert, and locally produced *aquavit.*"

Salmon fishing in these areas has been going on for a long time, and virtually all of it is privately controlled. In Norway, the rights to fish for salmon were granted by the old kings to farmers and are hereditary, passed on from generation to generation. Conservation can be a problem, with the farmers downriver, and especially at the mouths of rivers where nets may be strung. On the River A, one can see iron bolts dating perhaps to the Middle Ages in rocks where nets used to be tied and strung across the river. Another potential difficulty in Norway is a tendency, still muted, to develop wild water resources for hydroelectric and other commercial purposes.

NEW GUINEA

About as far away from Norway and old world fishing tradition as one can get is New Guinea, the home of aboriginal head-hunters, in the Pacific north of Australia.

Lefty Kreh is a former newspaperman, now professional fly-fishing lecturer, writer, film producer, casting instructor, and general fly-fishing innovator. He has fished just about anywhere one can fish with a fly rod, which is almost everywhere. He says of New Guinea, "This is the most exciting place I've fished with a fly rod. Most of the rivers have never been fished, at least for sport; the fish have never seen a lure, to say nothing of a fly, and they're the strongest fish in the world. Anybody who's caught one says so. Not that there are many of those. Maybe a hundred of these fish have been caught, and not more than a dozen on a fly rod.

"The fish is called the Nuigini black bass. N U I G I N I. That's how they spell it. It's of the Lutjanus genus. . . . No, it's not related to the peacock bass [a game fish that lives in South America]. If you tied a five-pound Nuigini bass to a twenty-five-pound peacock bass, the Nuigini bass would pull the peacock bass so fast, his scales would rip off. The Nuigini bass is also called the River Rambo. I like that.

"First time I was there, I was with some Australians I'd been hunting with in the Outback. The Australians are great practical jokers, you know. Well, they rigged up the night before on forty- and fifty-pound test line. I rigged up my fly rod on twenty-pound test tippet, the heaviest I've used anywhere. The next morning, when I saw that was all they put in the boat, I began to think maybe this wasn't a joke.

"We go out. The mate stops the boat near some fallen timber along the bank, but leaves the motor on, in neutral. One of the guys turns the drag [a braking system on large reels to slow down large fish] on his reel down until it's entirely shut. He casts this nine-inch plug with extra-strength steel treble hooks at the timber, lets it sink, and retrieves it. Out comes this big green thing. He shouts, 'Hit it, Dean!' Dean puts the motor in reverse. They're trying to tow this fish out of the timber! The line snaps with a loud crack. Well, I tie on the fifty-pound stuff. I'm using a twelve-weight rod with fifteen-weight fast-sinking line I use for sail fish.

"It's my turn. I throw out a big Lefty's Deceiver [a much-used fly Mr. Kreh designed to imitate saltwater bait fish]. A bass grabs it. I shout, 'Hit it, Dean!' The line tears out of the reel and burns a groove in my palm. It breaks. The next time, I wrap the line two times around the reel. That works. We tow the fish out to the open water where I can fight it. After a couple of minutes, it gives up. It only weighs twelve or thirteen pounds. I was amazed. What happens is they wait in sunken brush to ambush other fish, dart out, grab them, and dart back. On a lure, they use all their energy in a concentrated burst.

"No one knows how big these fish get. The biggest one caught was forty pounds. Once I had a small one on; an eighty-pounder came out of nowhere, grabbed it, and took off. The leader broke. They probably go over a hundred pounds."

Fishing is incredible offshore as well. "The water is beautiful," Lefty says. "It's the clearest water, and extremely deep. You can hook black marlin within two hundred yards of shore, and dog tooth tuna weighing sixty or eighty pounds, and baramundi. It's an absolute paradise for light tackle and fly-fishing."

Human life in New Guinea, as Lefty describes it, is unchanged from prehistoric times, although there hasn't been any cannibalism since World War II. "I feel safer walking into a village unannounced than walking down Fifth Avenue in Manhattan at night," Lefty says. "I find natives everywhere always open and ready to share. It seems that the further away from civilization you get, the friendlier the people are."

There are three ways to fish in New Guinea. One is to camp in tents, another is to stay at one of several Australian-managed hunting lodges, all of which are close to fishing areas, and the third is to take an Australian boat one can live aboard that anchors offshore but carries smaller boats to maneuver up the rivers. The cost of the latter, Lefty says, is not as much as some Alaskan trips; it's less than $3,000 for five or six fishing days. Air fares to New Guinea via Australia can be well under $1,000 if one makes arrangements far enough in advance. By contrast, the Hemingways' Norwegian trip, excluding travel, is about $4,000 per person, which for Norway is modest; the best beats on the best rivers at the best part of the season in that country cost five times that.

Of course, one need not necessarily go far or spend much money for reasonably good fly-fishing. Sometimes, it can be found surprisingly close to home.

10

BEST FISH

The first light cracked the darkness, a premonition of dawn. The likelihood was that the new day would be as gray as the previous one. The temperature was just above freezing, and the air was raw and damp; long underwear and outer layers of propylene and wool failed to ward off the chill.

Two fishermen upstream from me were barely discernible. We were waist-deep in waders in rushing forty-degree water. I saw the outlines of the others casting patiently and methodically albeit with an urgency I could detect by the quickness with which they picked up the line once the drift of the previous cast had ended, and recast. That urgency betrayed expectation. I experienced it as well.

Soon, the slowly lightening sky would show riverbanks of congealed mud with an overlay of decaying sticks and leaves, and behind a forest of barren hardwood trees, all in mono-chrome grays and browns. The scene brought to mind the last ring of Dante's *Inferno* where Lucifer himself oversees the worst sinners. This ring, unlike the others which are hot from fires, is frozen:

> Never did the Danube in Austria, nor the far-off Don under its cold sky, make in winter so thick a veil for cur-rent as was here.

An embellishment on the *Inferno* for us was the stench of large decaying salmon carcasses with eyeless heads and black-ened skin hanging on raw skeletons.

The place was a river tributary of Lake Ontario, one of the five Great Lakes. The time was late November, at the end of the run of coho salmon and the height of the steelhead run. Both species, as well as some large brown trout, spend their lives in the lake, becoming fat and healthy on oily alewives and other bait fish. In most other parts of the world, these fish mi-grate to and from the sea, most particularly the Pacific Ocean.

The coho salmon, unlike their Atlantic cousins, die fol-lowing the propagation and laying of eggs, which occurs when they're four years old. The hen salmon deposits the eggs by the thousands in nests both she and the male scoop out of gravel. The eggs are a gelatinous yellow almost the size of a standard glass marble. Many are loosened by the current, and float free as bait for steelhead trout.

Our game was the steelhead, a strong, sleek, hard-fighting variety of rainbow trout which has an instinct, like salmon, to migrate to the sea, or a large lake. Because of the greater abundance of food there, these fish grow considerably larger than their cousins, who remain where they were born. Their distinctive red stripe fades to a light, steely gray, which dark-ens somewhat once they are back in their natal river.

These sleek, powerful fish cruising like submarines about the carnage of the coho salmon, ingesting the salmon eggs whenever they find them, are a microcosm of the struggle for survival. The end of the predatory chain, however, was not the steelhead but us. We were hunting the hunters. Our ultimate weapon was knowing more about the fish than they did about us. We were pitting our cunning against their instinct to avoid danger. More often than not, they would win, either by avoiding our lures or shaking themselves loose once hooked. More often than not, fishermen leave the river empty-handed. Most fishermen use as lures actual salmon eggs, tied in small sacks to hooks, or imitation eggs in plastic or yarn, sometimes with scent added, sometimes even on a fly rod. Our flies were small but tied on stronger than normal hooks. They were designed as "attracters," representing nothing natural, and were tied to the ends of long leaders with small lead shots so they would sink in the strong, deep current. Our rigs had been assembled the evening before under electric light, so we wouldn't have to fiddle with knots in the cold, dark morning.

We'd not been in the river long when I saw the rod tip of Riccardo Azzoni, the angler upstream a few paces, take a fast dive. Then came the standard shout in large game fishing, "Fish on," which translates to a request, always complied with, for everyone with a line nearby to reel in so as to avoid tangles and a lost fish. I pulled my line in and backed up onto the shore. Riccardo passed in front of me, following his fish downriver. I recast. Wham!

A heavy fish connected with my line, too heavy, I could feel, for me to hold unless I moved, and moved fast. Otherwise, excess tension on the line would allow the fish to break the thin leader. Like Riccardo, I stumbled downriver under a bridge, following the fish, splashing in the water along the bank. As the fish was moving faster than me, I was allowing line to be released from the reel until there was almost none left. When the fish reached a large pool, about one hundred yards later, it slowed down to make its stand but thirty yards away at the opposite bank. It leapt into the air four times, showing an enormous bulk that sent a shiver of awe and also fear through me. At one heart-stopping moment, it swam under a large tree that had fallen into the water. In addition to the tree now, there was the problem of diminishing control with so much line out. Thinking fast, I dropped the rod tip so as to bring the line down to the surface. Miraculously, the line slipped under the branches. The fish churned about the surface, creating a wake that could have been caused by a washing machine in full cycle. Eventually the fish tired. Slowly, I coaxed it to my side of the river, wading out to meet it up to my knees.

From the corner of my eye, I saw Barry DeYulio, the trip leader whose family is known in the Stamford, Connecticut, area for the great sausage they pack. Wading knee-deep, a long-handled net in both hands, Barry came up behind me fast but quietly so as not to alarm the fish any more than it was. A couple of times I brought the fish close to Barry so he could slip the net under it, from behind, but somehow it sensed the new danger, found a reserve of power, and surged to the middle of the pool. Because of its weight, I had to let it go, and then induce it gently to return.

"Careful, now. . . . Take it easy. . . . Now, see if you can swing it over, gently," Barry coached me. The third time, Barry fitted the net right under the fish and, in one quick motion, raised the net, trapping the fish in the mesh. At that moment, for the first time since I'd hooked the fish, which seemed like an aeon ago, my heart rate slowed. A sense of peace overwhelmed me.

My elation continued, undiminished, during the six-hour drive home.

Another time, back home in Connecticut on Long Island Sound, I was on my bicycle checking the availability of lobsters with our one commercial lobsterman. He pointed to the cove in front of his dock. "See the bluefish?" he asked. I didn't. "Just look where the water is darker," he said. Then I saw.

It was a bluefish blitz. The darkness was the disruption of the water surface by hundreds of foot-long bunker that were frantically trying to escape an onslaught of bluefish attacking them from below. The bluefish is like a death machine. Even when blues are gorged and have no room to eat more, they cannot resist continuing to kill. Roving like wolf packs in search of prey, they can strike at virtually anything that moves. When they find a school of bunker, they herd it into a cove or up against a bank, and proceed to decimate the bunker, generally by chopping them in thirds with bear-trap-like jaws filled with small dagger-like teeth. They return to swallow the parts. The oil and parts from the bunker often attract gulls and other birds, which somehow know better than to land on the water until the blues leave. This devastation usually occurs at low tide; at other tides, more water is available to provide some of the school an escape route under or around the blues.

For years, I'd been awaiting this moment. I'd caught blues in a traditional way of trolling from a power boat, trailing wire lines with heavy metal lures at the end. Catching fish this way really isn't fun. Once hooked, they rarely escape, and in any event, there is little feeling of the fish; one might as well be hauling in a tire. The other standard way of catching blues is to cast and retrieve a lure. Alternatively, one can cast a chunk of bunker impaled on a hook into the water, set the rod into the sand, and wait for action at the far end of the line, also dull.

I'd long heard of fly-fishing in salt water, seen slide shows on the subject, and even read articles about it, but couldn't imagine doing it. The idea of casting some feathers tied to a hook into the sea with the expectation that a fish would be there to say nothing of its striking at the hook required an excess of faith. Eventually, my credulity expanded, and I began fishing for striped bass, a game fish so endangered that most Atlantic coast states limit takes to fish of over thirty-four inches, a very large bass. I'd caught some small stripers on flies, and found them to be good, strong fish but still not as dramatic as the blues, mostly because they don't jump. Except for their size, catching one in open water without rocks, trees, currents, or other impediments is pretty much like catching another; there are no impediments to complicate and battle and make it more interesting.

I thanked the lobsterman, sprang back on my bicycle, peddled back home as fast as I could, shoved my saltwater fly-fishing gear into the car, and raced back. To my relief, the blitz was continuing. I pulled on my waders and jumped into the cove. Having picked oysters there before at low tide, I knew what to expect—soft, oozing mud. Slowly, sinking into the mud sometimes up to my knees, and occasionally, when I slipped, cutting a hand on edges of oyster shells embedded in the mud, I made my way, step by step, toward the blitz, frustrated by the delay and fearful that the blues would leave. Eventually I reached casting distance of the blitz. It formed a continually shifting circle of some ten yards in diameter. I could see better what was happening, the fins and tails of the bunker showing with the backs of their much larger pursuers.

With some trepidation, aware that blues can slash at human legs, I cast into the blitz, again and again. I backed up when the blitz approached me, the blues driving the bunker from the opposite end, and followed it when it moved away from me. The goal was to induce one of these creatures to strike my clutch of bright yellow feathers designed to imitate a six-inch bait fish, not so simple a task when there was so much real prey around twice that length. In due course, one bit. I felt a heavy tug at the end of the line. The blue, angry that his gorging had been interrupted, took off, leaping into the air again and again, crashing down on the water.

Fortunately, the blue's teeth didn't get beyond the steel shank of the hook to cut the leader, and after a while it slowed down. The question became, "What to do next?" Most blues fishermen carry gaffs with which to hook the fish in the gills; they don't place fingers near the fishes' teeth. Puzzling this, I backed up slowly with the fish at the end of the line, until I reached shore, and then pulled it by the line gingerly onto the stones so there was little room for it to maneuver. There was no choice then. Watching its jaws, I slipped my fingers into the gills as unobtrusively as I could, and flung the fish the rest of the way onto the stone beach. I was flooded by a sense of both relief, at having captured a blue on a fly rod, and triumph, unadulterated in this instance by any sadness at having witnessed the single-minded havoc the blue and its brethren had wreaked on the bunker.

In both catches, wit and intuition had overcome lack of experience, either my own or someone else's. Catching my first Atlantic salmon, although it brought tears of gratitude to my eyes, was not the same; then I had a guide next to me, placing me in the right spots, choosing flies, and when the fish struck, instructing my almost every move. The achievement of the steelhead and blue catches was mine alone. In both instances, I was at one with the natural world, competing with these other, alien creatures of God, every one of my senses alert, using instinct passed on from aeons past as well as intelligence. I was very much alive.

11

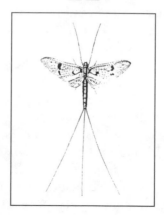

BETTER FLY-FISHING

The love of fly-fishing is shared by more people than most of us realize. The role the sport plays in each of our lives varies, of course, but the most committed take it upon themselves to return something to the sport, for their own satisfaction and the benefit of others who may never know of their contribution. In some cases, their efforts require not only imagination but courage.

This chapter examines three examples in which fisheries have been pulled back from the brink of destruction, or may be in the process of having that happen. They are examples, too, of what is possible in a democratic society when individuals want change enough to buck the greed or ineptitude of others.

CALIFORNIA TROUT

In California in the nineteen-sixties, trout fisheries policy was to provide anglers with as many "catchable" trout as state hatcheries could produce. State fisheries managers, with the concurrence of the legislators who approved funding, decided that this was what California anglers wanted.

"Hatcheries were built; fish were bred, hybridized and degraded, and dumped into rivers and streams to satisfy an apparently insatiable demand by anglers to fill their creels every fishing trip," says Richard May, one of the founders of California Trout, a private, nonprofit organization. Success was measured in numbers of fish caught per "angling hour," somewhat similar to the body count measures of progress in the Vietnam war, which was then heating up. Anglers were led to expect more fish, and then demanded bigger and better fish. The hatcheries could provide large numbers of fish but not quality; hatchery fish, in Mr. May's words, are "poor performers, worse survivors, and inferior cuisine."

Dr. Brian Curtis was among a few California anglers, biologists, and environmentalists who had another idea, the protection of wild trout, defined as trout hatched naturally in the stream in which they are born, with no stocking and, if necessary, no killing. Dr. Curtis, now deceased, was a wealthy environmentalist married to a Lithuanian princess. In midlife in the nineteen-fifties, he obtained advanced degrees in biology at Stanford. He joined the California Department of Fish and Game and then Pacific Gas & Electric. PG&E, many of whose senior management were members of the Sierra Club, was committed to the then nascent environmental protection movement. One of the state's major users of hydropower, PG&E also had more resources than the state agencies to fund fisheries studies, especially Dr. Curtis's special interest:

the effect of water flow reductions on fisheries. Dr. Curtis passed his ideas on wild trout management to Dr. James Adams, another PG&E biologist, who took it upon himself to see that they were implemented.

"There was a real ethic at PG&E then to do the right thing," Dr. Adams says. "The Fish and Game Department saw no merit to the program. PG&E would have taken on the whole project, but I thought we should bring in others. That caused a lot of agony but in the long run, of course, it was right."

After selling PG&E on the idea of testing the viability of managing a fishery for the propagation of wild trout in 1964, Dr. Adams combined forces with California Trout. One of the members was Mr. May. "This was a whole new thrust, managing water for wild trout," Mr. May said. "There was no reluctance individually at the highest government levels but the agencies overall were anything but progressive. We saw local, citizen initiative as the way to go."

Before formally approaching the authorities for approval of policy and regulation changes, CalTrout wanted proof that the idea would work, namely that "put and take" fishing could be successfully supplanted by a "catch and release" practice. Dr. Adams brought them plans for two tests.

The site of the first was a lake in Shasta County in northern California. CalTrout, PG&E, and Department of Fish and Game personnel hauled gravel to the lake, into which hatchery-bred trout had to be periodically dumped. They placed the gravel in the outflow of the lake. Within a few weeks, large egg- and milt-filled trout were hovering over the gravel. A spawning bed had been created. The reason for the lack of a self-sustaining trout population was simply that there had been no spawning area; the hatchery truck, theoretically, at least, was no longer necessary.

The next test was more ambitious. The site was a three-and-one-half-mile stretch of nearby Hat Creek, a crystal-clear stream that bubbles out of springs fed by the snows of volcanic Mount Lassen and flows through rolling mid-elevation grasslands and groves of pine and fir. Suckers and squawfish, considered trash fish, had all but crowded out the trout natural to the area.

Four parties entered into an agreement. The state Wildlife Conservation Board was to provide funding for a barrier at the lower end of the test site to stop trash fish from moving upstream. PG&E said it would grant the state title to the barrier area, permit public access to the stream above the barrier, and provide some more funding. The Department of Fish and Game agreed to temporarily remove the few wild trout left in the test area, poison the other fish, stock the stream with the remaining indigenous trout and other specially selected trout, and then manage the stream as a premium, wild trout fishery with special regulations, including reduced bag limits, that would assure that the trout population would sustain itself with no further stocking. CalTrout was to raise funds for graduate fisheries students at Humboldt State College to evaluate the results of the program for five years, funds which subsequently were matched by Humboldt.

The results confirmed two assumptions: the stream was amazingly productive, though its demise as a wild trout fishery was nearly complete. Over 12,600 pounds of trash fish, mostly suckers, were removed from the stream compared to 321 pounds of trout. Without the competition of the trash fish, the newly stocked trout and their progeny could thrive.

Five years later, with data from the Humboldt grad students in hand, CalTrout proposed to the Fish and Game Commission the adoption of two trout management programs, each with different objectives. One was to leave the management of heavily fished areas near cities and public parks as it was, and the other was to manage the balance as wild trout and steelhead fisheries. CalTrout defines the wild fish policy as "management so that natural populations of fish . . . will be virtually unaffected by angling mortality or habitat degradation." The proposal was accepted and later formalized by the state legislature. At present, forty California rivers, streams, and lakes are managed as wild trout and steelhead waters, with no stocking and severe limitations on keeping fish.

Subsequent changes were made to Hat Creek, including placing boulders and large tree trunks as cover for larger fish, the introduction of some aquatic grasses, restoration of stream banks, and restrictions on cattle grazing. The trout population has stabilized at what's considered a norm of twenty thousand fish, some of which grow very large.

CalTrout has moved on to other somewhat less dramatic but equally important projects, including the encouragement of changes in land management practices in national forests to limit clear cutting, the inclusion of state waters for protection in the National Wild and Scenic Rivers System, and negotiation and litigation to induce other hydropower companies to release water from dams to either protect or make possible trout fisheries.

"California is at the cutting edge nationally of wild trout management, and Hat Creek is where it all began," Mr. May says. "It's about citizens changing history."

ATLANTIC COAST STRIPED BASS

Not long ago, Atlantic coast striped bass were close to extinction. They've come back. Every season, one finds larger, more frequent, and more predictable catches. On every successful fishing trip, one is filled with gratitude. If a longtime Atlantic Coast fly-fisher didn't know what had been happening, he might consider the recovery a miracle. However, the return of the striped bass is the result of two decades of concerted effort by hundreds of individuals—members of state and federal fisheries agencies, sportsmen's clubs, political groups, private foundations, and concerned citizens—who have pitted their foresight, dedication, technical abilities, research, political acumen, and an enormous amount of time and money against ignorance and fear of the unknown.

Striped bass are an American legacy. A journal in 1637 reported that "such multitudes passe out of a pounde that it seemed that one might go over their backs drishod." Yet even then, the fishery was exploited to the point that, two years later, the General Court in Boston, in the first fishing regulation in the New World, prohibited their use as fertilizer for corn and squash plantings. Subsequent taxes on catches of the fish helped build America's first public school. Legislated fisheries management also goes back a long way. In the first year of the Revolution, the legislatures of New York and Massachusetts suspended their efforts to raise money for George Washington's army long enough to ban winter-time commercial fishing for striped bass. The importance of the fish is further noted by Larry Simms, president of the Maryland Waterman's Association, the purpose of which is to protect the interests of the state's commercial shell and fin fishermen. He says, "Look at the Maryland state seal. It's got a shield with an individual on each side. One is a farmer; the other is a waterman holding a fish, and the fish has stripes!"

Striped bass are a remarkable fish, capable of living as long as thirty years and growing to six feet in length, although these days bass more than four feet long are scarce. Nonetheless, bass the size of average salmon and occasionally larger are caught now, even wading alongside rocks or sea grass from shore with a fly rod. Most of these fish live their early lives in areas where they couldn't be more vulnerable to human depredation—the estuaries of the Chesapeake Bay and New York City harbor, and to a lesser extent those along the Virginia and North Carolina coasts. Those that survive hooks, nets, and pollution migrate to the ocean, where they are safer, probably happier, and can grow really large.

Despite the hellish urban sights, smells, and noise surrounding the waters where bass are born and spend their early years, it's not difficult to imagine them as pristine. In 1609, Robert Juet, aboard the *Half Moon* captained by Henry Hudson, wrote, "This is a very good Land to fall with and a pleasant Land to see." Juet and the *Half Moon* crew saw a very different Hudson River from the one we see. At the time, broad shoals and wetlands constituted the river's banks. Yet as early as 1700, most of Manhattan's riverbanks had been bulkheaded, and since then almost three hundred square miles of harbor bottom and marshes have been converted to dry land for use as wharfs, storage depots, housing, highways, and three international airports.

"I was killing a hundred rockfish [the Cheaspeake Bay area name for striped bass] a day when they were running," says Philip Krista, a convert to conservation who now guides fly-fishermen for striped bass on the Patapsco River, which flows into Baltimore Harbor. The river was also treated as a God-given sewer. "In Oella, we had cable TV before we had flush toilets," Mr. Krista says. "Everything would end up in the river. The water would change color sometimes every day, depending upon what dyes the mills upstream had too much of." Others were catching the bass for sale to restaurants in Balti-more, Washington, and elsewhere. In the nineteen-eighties, the warning signs became loud and clear. Striped bass catches were dropping precipitously. The commercial harvest in 1983 amounted to three and a half million pounds, down from a high ten years earlier of nearly fifteen million pounds. (Catches by anglers were estimated at about the same as the commercial catches.)

The question was, "What to do?" There were two basic problems, Bill Goldsborough of the Chesapeake Bay Foun-dation explained. The first had to with a debate as to the cause of decline of the striped bass fishery. Could it be due to habitat degradation through pollution, in particular water over the spawning grounds? Or was it simply overfishing? The resolution was to agree that the decline in the striped bass population "can be halted or reversed by a reduction in fish-ing mortality, even if contaminant toxicity is the proximate cause."

A second debate centered on determining who was to blame for the overfishing. Chesapeake Bay fishermen blamed New England fishermen for catching large spawners, and the New Englanders pointed the finger at the southerners for taking immature fish. State fisheries departments' jurisdic-tions were limited to their own states, while the fish, which migrate from Cape Hatteras in North Carolina to the Bay of Fundy in New Brunswick, don't recognize such boundaries. The Atlantic States Marine Fisheries Commission (ASMFC), a creature of fifteen Atlantic coast states, had produced a lot of fine-sounding recommendations that were for the most part ignored. The burden of dealing with this regulatory nightmare was shifted to Congress, which in 1984 passed a law that compelled the states to implement the commission's striped bass restoration plan. Congress gave the commission enforcement powers. Over the next two years, under pressure to do what heretofore was politically impossible, the affected states banned outright the keeping of striped bass.

By 1995, two decades later, the bass population from the Cheaspeake Bay area was deemed recovered, recovery being defined in technical terms by the ASMFC as the existence of sufficient "spawning stock biomass" (SSB). SSB is the estimated weight of sexually mature females in a population, as determined by returns of tags clipped on fish and other data.

Without sufficient numbers of spawners and mates, a species cannot reproduce enough to offset natural loss, and becomes doomed to extinction. Once-plentiful cod, herring, turbot, sturgeon, and some salmon, a source of protein to millions as well as sport, face this danger. The goal for the striped bass now is to ensure that the recovered spawning stock is allowed to maintain itself at rates equal to the highs of three decades ago.

Paul Perra, former program director for the ASMFC, now with the National Marine Fisheries Service, says, "It took a lot of courage for state fisheries directors to push this through. They laid their jobs on the line." Pressure was placed on state governors to kill the legislation, and fishermen in Virginia even hired a lobbyist to influence a "nay" vote in the Congress.

The plan continues to attract opposition. Much of it comes from sport fishermen, especially in the New York area, who are pleased with the results of the plan and would like to have commercial fishing rights limited or even banned. The Virginia state legislature has enacted a law that threatens to repeal its compact with the ASMFC; two other states are considering the same move. The issue comes down to one of subrogation of states rights to another authority.

Without the same attention, the Pacific striped bass have fared worse. Those bass are descendants of four hundred and thirty-five yearling fish, netted in the Hudson River in 1879 and 1881 and hauled by rail car to California to replace the salmon that had been decimated by overfishing and the use of their spawning waters to wash gold from ore. The bass thrived. Moreover, they were easy to catch. Unlike their Atlantic coast cousins, they didn't roam. Cold water temperatures kept them close to San Francisco and other Bayside communities. In 1899, the commercial catch totaled 1,234,000 pounds. The numbers now are way down, and dropping further every year. The culprit in this case is neither overfishing nor pollution but irrigation. Fresh water is being diverted from the San Francisco Bay/Delta area in enormous quantities through canals to irrigate, at taxpayer expense, cotton fields in the Central Valley. The suction of the two pumping stations is strong enough to reverse tides, confusing bass trying to spawn and killing an estimated two hundred million offspring of the fish that succeed in spawning, and even greater numbers of larvae. Congress intervened in this case as well with legislation requiring the partial restoration of freshwater flows. It's too soon to know whether the legislation will help.

In the East, protection of the hard-won gains for the striped bass fishery involves the efforts of a vast array of private organizations and citizen volunteers. One of them, the 6,000–member American Littoral Society monitors wetlands and water quality. The society also coordinates a program whereby fishermen tag fish they catch and release them. When the fish are recaught, the tags are removed by the next fisherman and mailed to the society, which passes them on to the ASMFC and other interested parties. Sometimes the fishermen slip a note into the envelope along with the tag. Anthony Anastasio of Holbrook, Massachusetts, a retired carpenter, wrote, "I am returning this tag I was lucky enough to catch in a striped bass . . . at Hingham MA. The fish was 23 lbs. and 37 1/2 inches long. I was going to eat this fish, but it looked too good to eat so I gave it a big kiss and wished it all the luck in the world."

THE BIG BLACKFOOT

This story of the rescue of the Big Blackfoot in Montana isn't concluded. The valley through which the 120-mile long river runs is the setting of Norman Maclean's book *A River Runs Through It*. However, the movie that followed was filmed on the Gallatin and Yellowstone rivers; the fishery on Big Blackfoot had been devastated by too much mining, logging, livestock grazing, and fishing. Three people took it upon themselves to reverse the degradation of the river. Against opposition that included threats to their property and even lives, they garnered increasing support that is showing results. However, the threat to the river continues in one form or another, the current one being a proposal to create near its headwaters an enormous open pit gold mine which may leak cyanide and still more poisons into the Big Blackfoot.

The catalyst for citizen action was a similar plan propounded in 1987 by the Dallas-based Sunshine Mining Company. Sunshine would have stripped a substantial part of the Blackfoot landscape, piled ore two hundred yards from the river, and dripped cyanide through it to leach out the gold. The Big Blackfoot is home to an unusual strain of Westcoast cutthroat trout and also the rare bull trout, which grows to more than twenty pounds when its habitat is left alone. Near the proposed Sunshine mine site was a small ranch owned by S. Daryl Parker, a California industrial contractor who had moved to Lincoln, a town with a population of 1,000, to be able to regularly fish the Big Blackfoot. Of the Sunshine project, Mr. Parker says, "My wife and I decided to organize a few people to bring this to the public's attention." He adds modestly, "I was a small part of this overall desire to restore and protect the Big Blackfoot."

Mr. Parker's idea was to organize the drive within a new Trout Unlimited chapter that would allow local citizen initiative to attract state and national backing. His nucleus comprised two others. Becky Garland, mother of two, part-time mother of three more, and proprietor of a Lincoln general store, says, "Daryl called me up one day and said, 'I'm putting you on the board as vice president.' I don't have much time to fish, but he knew I was interested. I'd been involved in Earth Day and the Wilderness Association, and I'm Cecil Garland's daughter." Cecil Garland, the store's prior owner, spent most of Becky's childhood campaigning for the creation of the Scapegoat Wilderness north of Lincoln that connects with two other wilderness areas and Glacier National Park to form the premier ecosystem in the lower forty-eight. "He was away, or on the phone, or people were over," Ms. Garland says. "There really was not a lot of talk about anything else. Sure, I was influenced. It's a caretaker kind of thing. It's our gift. I'm taking care of my part of Mother Earth. The watershed of the Big Blackfoot is my big picture. It's all I've known. I want to make sure it remains for my children." Mr. Garland sustained his efforts through a boycott of his store by his neighbors, and after eleven years, Congress approved the inclusion of the area in the national Wilderness system.

Mark Gerlach, who works for a ranching partnership, was enlisted by Mr. Parker as well and is the current chapter president. Mr. Gerlach doesn't fish much, but he'd lobbied in the state capital and had been otherwise involved in environmental issues, especially over cutting in the National Forests. To remain effective, he'd avoided affiliation with any organization; many Montanans are suspicious of out-of-state organizations that don't promise cash or jobs. Trout Unlimited appeared to Mr. Gerlach to be a middle-of-the-road sportsman's group. Others didn't like what the Big Blackfoot chapter was doing. "Sunshine literally lobbied in the bars," Mr.

Gerlach says. "They promised people forty thousand–dollar jobs, new roads and schools, and people believed them. No matter that they'd be gone in a few years, leaving a gaping, enormous hole in the earth and a polluted river. I'd get real profane calls in the middle of the night. I didn't know who they were. Once, a guy I knew came up to me and said, 'You environmental asshole, I'm going to shoot your ass.' I answered, 'You better shoot straight 'cause all you're going to get is one shot.' "

Digging for data, chapter members found that Sunshine had been cited for eighty-five water quality violations at a silver mine in nearby Idaho. The information was publicized in Montana. Not much has been heard about the proposal since.

In the meantime, the chapter commenced work on reversing the damage to the Big Blackfoot fishery. Officials from state and federal fisheries, forestry and land management agencies, and interested citizens, in particular ranchers, were brought together; a study was made of the difficulties the fishery faced; a plan was prepared; agreements were reached with private landholders; and more than $1,000,000 was raised privately to supplement about half that amount in public funds. Initial funding mostly from individuals in the watershed was followed by grants from a myriad of small environmental conservation foundations, the Orvis Company, national Trout Unlimited, and Robert Redford, who donated the proceeds of the Livingston, Montana, opening of *A River Runs Through It*.

The main job was to convince the property holders in the valley of the value of cleaning up the river. That happened, allowing work to begin. Improvements are being concentrated on the river's eighty tributaries, where spawning and rearing of the young Big Blackfoot trout occur. Under way are fence building to keep cattle from trampling the stream banks, tree planting along the banks, replacing culverts which impede stream flow with bridges, and digging new channels where fish are denied access to stream headwaters. A lot of this work requires the rental of track hoes and other equipment at costs of up to $200 an hour. Also under way is work with the owners of mines—the ugly red-colored liquid toxins from just one having caused an eight-mile zone that creeps downriver a little farther every year, depressing aquatic life along the way—and with multinational timber corporations to change cutting practices that denude whole mountain slopes, causing sediments as well as toxins to be washed into the tributary streams and river. Regulations also have been amended, prohibiting the killing of the Westslope cutthroat and bull trout, limiting takes of rainbow and brown trout to three fish under twelve inches, and changing the seasons during which fishing is permitted.

Already there are results. "Populations have increased one hundred percent in the main stem," Don Peters of the Department of Fish, Wildlife and Parks says. Ms. Garland adds, "We physically count the redds, which are the spawning beds, in the tributaries. Where there were one or two in places before we started working, there are now fifteen. It's as dramatic as that."

The environmentalists fear that the latest threat could undo all that's been done to date, and more. The project is propounded by a partnership of Phelps Dodge in Phoenix and Canyon Resources in Goldon, Colorado, named the Seven-Up Pete Joint Venture (SPJV). SPJV's goal over the next fifteen or so years is to recover from four hundred acres of state and private land nearly four million ounces of gold. To do so, it would dig a hole nearly a mile around and more than one thousand feet deep a half mile from the Big Blackfoot upriver from Lincoln. One billion tons of earth and rock would be dug from the pit. A portion of that would be leached, or soaked, with recirculated cyanide to separate the gold from the ore. The technology, the company says, is well established, state-of-the-art, and environmentally sound. The opponents note a sad history in Montana and elsewhere of spills and leaks from similar "heap leach" gold mines, which have polluted once-clean waters.

"We've never seen this technology prevent the pollution of

surace and ground water," Geoff Smith, staff scientist of the Clark Fork–Pend Oreille Coalition, a citizen's environmental organization with offices in Montana and Idaho, says of the heap leach process. "It works at recovering gold, but not at protecting water quality." Mr. Smith sees eventual pollution to the Big Blackfoot through drainage from the mined rock of acid, nitrates, and ammonia, and cyanide leakage from the leach pads, which can be punctured and torn.

Mike Schern, manager of the SPJV, responds, "We will only develop this project in a way which will protect the environment. The rocks at MacDonald [the pit area] do not produce acid and the final pit lake will be fresh enough to support a stocked fishery . . . We have very carefully studied the local environment and know more about this part of the Blackfoot Valley than anyone, and we're sharing that knowledge with the public through the environmental impact study process."

The process to which Mr. Schern refers is embodied in SPJV's ten-thousand-page, thirty-one-volume application for a mining permit. Analysis and approval of the application is required of seventeen state and federal agencies, the first and most important of which is the Hard Rock Bureau of the Montana Department of State Lands. Although a preliminary review of the application led the bureau to pose 750 questions to SPJV, the environmentalists wonder how rigorous the bureau's follow-up will be. The mandate of some of these agencies is narrow, and the environmentalists question the extent to which they will consider how the mine might affect the river and valley. Moreover, the record of the Hard Rock Bureau, and also its sister Water Quality Division, isn't encouraging. An audit of the Hard Rock Bureau by the Montana legislature uncovered long delays in mandated mine inspections, failure to cite violations, failure to enforce correction of those that had been cited, and reduction of fines to levels a small fraction of amounts provided by policy. Department Commissioner Bud Clinch says he welcomed the audit, and most of the suggestions have been implemented.

It's not difficult to understand the appeal of the project to the state and the community. It would create 390 jobs paying an average of $36,000 each, a large amount in that part of the country. In addition, the venture would purchase about a half billion dollars' worth of goods and services, many from the area, and would throw off large royalty payments, the beneficiary of which is the University of Montana, and pay even more in federal, state, and local taxes.

"You can't continue to extract resources in this valley," Mr. Gerlach says. "To live here, you make a choice between quality of life and standard of living. You can't have both; here they're mutually exclusive. . . . Those guys aren't going to add to the quality of life here. They have another value system. They say there's $1.68 billion of gold in the earth here. They ask if the river is worth more than that. I say there's no price for the river."

As encouraging as these examples may be, they should be placed in perspective. "For every river or bay or estuary that is being cared for and has friends and funding, there are fifty that aren't," say Peter Rafle, editor of *Trout,* a magazine published by Trout Unlimited.

Mr. Rafle adds, "Across the country, there are thousands of people working to bring streams back, sometimes from true disaster. But they are a tiny fraction of the literally millions who take pleasure from fishing. I think every person who has caught a wild fish has a duty to give something back— either through volunteer work or by supporting one of the many organizations working to protect and restore fragile fisheries."

12

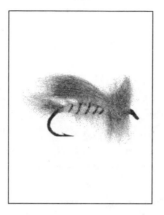

THE FUTURE

At a fishing camp in Maine patronized for generations by the same Boston families, I met a ninety-year-old retired blind physician. Undaunted by his disability and still in love with fly-fishing, he used to hire a guide to take him out on the lake in a boat. The guide directed the physician's casts. "There's a rise four feet out and a little to the left," the guide might have said. "Oops, the fish moved. . . . Try just a little closer. . . . Right on! You got him!"

To me as a young man, this man was a wonderment of courage and perseverance. When he showed up in the main lodge for breakfast, he and the guide discussed strategy for the day, and at dinner, he unobtrusively reviewed the results with a few guests. He appeared content and not at all self-conscious. He also provided me some consolation: Should infirmity strike me in my advanced years, I need not necessarily abandon my favorite pastime. Now that fewer fishing years are ahead of me than behind, I think of him more often, picturing him casting into a beautiful sunset, trout rises all around, none of which he could see, but anticipating the jolt to his arm of the strike on a trout at the end of his line.

Could he be me years hence, perhaps with Denise substituting for the guide? Is that my future? Or will some other infirmity strike, complicating in some other way the pursuit of my sport? Or indeed, will there be any fly-fishing at all in my old age, and if so, will it mean for others what it has meant for me?

Fly-fishing in my dotage and beyond will be affected by changes to the ecology; crowding on fishing waters; commercialization of the sport; the introduction to fly-fishing of persons unattuned to its spirit; dealing with the urge for proof of success, usually manifested in dead fish counts; and the graduation from that stage to a quest for joy and possibly significance.

Two ecological movements are vying with each other to shape the future of fly-fishing. One is for an improvement in the ecology in general and in fly-fishing in particular through better knowledge of trout and the management of their habitats. This movement is still fragile and susceptible to reversal. Its success will require political pressure backed by technical and, unfortunately, legal expertise and political clout. An ecology that can support improved fisheries also requires sacrifice, especially in the acceptance by property owners of limitations on revenue. Individual anglers must forgo the age-old habit of killing their catch; this, fortunately, appears to be increasingly accepted as a necessity of our times. The opposing trend, also under way and gaining momentum, is an assault on the regulations that have helped clean the environment to the point that fish can live in places where before they couldn't. Some environmental regulations cause undue hardship, but they can be modified; they need not be dumped wholesale.

"The wind that has been at the back of the environmentalists has now shifted one hundred and eighty degrees," said Stanley Bryer, president of Theodore Gordon Flyfishers, a New York–based conservation group. "The pendulum has swung in the opposite direction. We're being told that these environmental regulations 'hinder productivity and stifle economic growth.' The new political establishment has branded the [New York State] Department of Environmental Conservation as the agency that punishes business and treats profit seekers with contempt. Much of what we have fought for is suddenly at risk."

Still, at least small progress remains possible. My local Trout Unlimited chapter initiated a plan with the subsequent guidance of the Connecticut Department of Environmental Protection to change regulations on the small stream we had adopted. The stream is not notable except that it is within thirty miles of New York City, and thanks partly to its being a source of municipal drinking water, it's clean and cold enough to support trout. For three years, we conducted water quality tests, fish counts, and angler surveys, and testified before the legislature. Ultimately, fishing was permitted with artificial single-hooked lures, outside the normal April to October season, with all fish caught then to be released unharmed. The DEP also gave the stream a Class A rating, assuring it of prime attention.

"We were amazed this could be done," Phil Murphy III, the chapter president at the time, reminisced. "We knew what a great resource we had. The DEP really wasn't aware of it."

A fish ladder was built over the dam that blocks the flow of water into Long Island Sound and eventually the Atlantic. Colonial records indicate that salmon once came up the stream; now herring which like salmon are anadromous, have returned. Striped bass and bluefish poised on the sea side of the dam snatch the herring on their return to the sea. More exciting, some shad and even sea-run trout have been spotted struggling up the ladder into the stream. The idea of salmon returning, while farfetched, is theoretically possible someday.

To protect the now more usable fishery, the chapter has turned its attention to the entire watershed, whence have come chemicals of one kind and another, including lawn fertilizers and insecticides, that have killed fish, and equally deadly droughts, caused partly by the privately owned water company's sales to municipalities other than the one it's supposed to serve. A softening enforcement of regulations easily could cause this stream to revert to a warm, dirty water holdover for suckers, chub, and sunfish. "To see what we've done unravel because of a change in the political climate would be really sad," Mr. Murphy said.

Eventually, as the connections between different aspects of the environment becomes clearer, will our attention be focused still farther away, to the Connecticut legislature in Hartford or the Congress in Washington or worldwide ecological conferences? That seems likely.

In the meantime, the need for effective political action is resulting in the formation of more grass-roots conservation organizations like California Trout and the Clark Fork–Pend Oreille Coalition in Montana and Idaho. These groups, with mandates to protect and enhance specific watersheds, are assuming a greater role relative to the large, national conservation groups. The latter seem in the view of some to be increasingly dominated by lawyers who concentrate on larger, more global issues. Some of the smaller groups are able to obtain funding from conservation-oriented foundations to hire biologists to evaluate and contest the environmental impact statements required of developers. These groups understand the legal and legislative systems, to say nothing of knowing judges and legislators, often on a first-name basis. They can be tough adversaries to developers.

A dissenting view on the effectiveness of citizen-led conservation groups comes from Dr. Thomas Lovejoy of The Smithsonian Institution in Washington. "In the end," Dr. Lovejoy said, "conservation will require a comprehensive ecosystem approach. In the absence of ecosystem management, individual good efforts are likely to be overwhelmed by factors beyond their local control."

Acknowledging the very considerable progress that has been made since the first Earth Day in 1970, Carol Browner, administrator of the Environmental Protection Agency in Washington, noted that 40 percent of the rivers, streams, and lakes in the United States are not fit for fishing or even swimming, and that state health departments have issued advisories on more than one thousand lakes and rivers, warning people not to eat fish they catch there.

A different threat to the enjoyment of fly-fishing is the current faddishness of the sport. The often-photographed scene of anglers shoulder to shoulder, surrounding a freshly stocked roadside pool the first days of the season, long accepted in the East, is occurring now in the West. Fishing in popular spots on the Madison River in Montana is in February as it used to be in July. It's probably just a matter of time before fishing from the popular drift boats of the big Western rivers will take on the same anxiety that hot, grouchy, country-bound office workers feel in scrambling to escape from Manhattan island on a summer Friday evening, thousands of cars squeezing into the two- or three-lane streets leading to the bridges and tunnels.

Safety valves exist. The most obvious is for an angler just to move to less accessible water, which—for the time being, anyway—can be found. Another is the existence of an etiquette that permits fly-fishers to tolerate each other in what may be considered competitive situations. Generally, fly-fishers know what constitutes disturbing another fly-fisher, particularly the minimum distance one can stand next to another to cast, which depends in turn on the clarity, depth, and flow of the water—in other words, how easily the fish are disturbed. Crowds don't necessarily reduce catches, especially where fish must be released. Ironically, aquatic insect propagation and water temperature in some man-made tail waters, like the Green in Utah and San Juan in New Mexico, are so favorable to trout that nothing seems to upset their feeding.

When one is distracted by the presence of other anglers and has to maneuver for a reasonable position on the water, one's sense of peace and solitude is upset. In due course, the small streams some fly-fishers are seeking, myself included, will be discovered by others and they'll become popular as well. In time, the primary recourse for quality fly-fishing in relative solitude, outside of traveling to other continents, will become the leasing of rights to fish private water such as the Montana spring creeks. This is an occurrence Theodore Gordon predicted with foreboding but which at least has been delayed a century.

As for the Furies of commerce released by *A River Runs Through It,* they are disturbing to anglers accustomed to a time when assaults on the pocketbook were lower key and more easily ignored. Nonetheless, these furies are relatively benign, the producers of fishing goods and services being for the most part fly-fishermen themselves and averse to glitz. Moreover, pressure is likely to be limited not so much by pocketbook size as anglers' time—time to study, comprehend, and actually use increasingly sophisticated varieties of gear, lures, and accessories.

In the meantime, fly-fishing equipment manufacturers are enjoying a boom. No good data are available, most of the manufacturers being privately held companies not required to make public their financial statements. However, they are pushing goods out the door as fast as productive capacity can be increased, evidently at large and growing profit margins.

One manufacturer is so sanguine about profitability that it is offering a 100 percent lifetime guarantee on its rods. Equipment lines, too, are being expanded with more and more variety, as the ubiquitous, alluring, and ever-fattening catalogs show.

What about the Ralph Lauren anglers? They are apt to cause little more than a fading ripple on the fly-fishing scene. The enchantment of fly-fishing, like much else of value, is not for purchase. After some attempts at casting that never resemble those of the brothers in *A River Runs Through It;* flies hooked in streamside branches; mosquito or black fly bites and other frustrations that cannot be cured by cash or credit card, the $2,000 cane rods in tooled leather cases will come out of BMW trunks and quietly vanish in attic closets. Perhaps years hence, they'll be joyously discovered, if they haven't warped in the meantime, by a grandchild with a love for fishing, not appearances.

What challenges remain for those committed fly-fishers who need to break new ground? Many of the obvious feats seem to have been performed. Lee Wulff caught large salmon on a small dry fly and then without a rod. He even found a way to dispense with net or gaff. It does not seem that flies can be made any smaller than they are now or equipment any lighter and finer, or casts made any farther. Enormous tarpon, tuna, and sail fish have been caught on fly rods and with increasingly delicate leaders. Virtually every freshwater game fish seems to have been lured to a fly. Do fly-fishing frontiers remain?

For those fly-fishers who need to measure success by statistics, records for large fish always will be available to be topped. The record tarpon caught on a fly rod with the requisite strip of twelve-pound test leader is 188 pounds. Who is to say that a 190- or 200-pound tarpon isn't waiting somewhere to snatch some fortunate angler's fly? Maybe one already has. A growing number of anglers are constrained, to their credit, by a need to let sport fish live, and records must be confirmed by an impartial source, who can obviously weigh only fish that have been killed. There are indications from photographs that larger-than-record tarpon and steelhead have been caught but they were returned to the water to be caught again, or not, by other anglers.

Geographic frontiers for fly-fishing are fast diminishing but nonetheless remain. One fly-fishing trip organizer reportedly is exploring Mongolia for possibilities. Wealthy, seasoned anglers who have fished the usual far-off haunts of New Zealand and Argentina for trout and Iceland for salmon are offered trips now to catch sail fish and small marlin on flies in the Pacific off Costa Rica, peacock bass in the Amazon basin in Brazil, and salmon in Siberia.

The definition of the word "exotic" changes, as what was exotic yesterday becomes commonplace tomorrow. Anglers in search of the new and strange have no repose; they must stay on the move, but they do not always need to move far. Some anglers are seeking the exotic in trips to Canada to fish exclusively for pike or muskies. Heretofore, traditional fly-fishers have considered these giant predators unworthy of their attentions, probably because they are not especially selective in what they choose to ingest. What's needed to catch them are primarily the knack of knowing where to find them; a selection of large, gaudy flies to induce them from their lairs, often in weeds or sunken underbrush; and a strong arm. Closer still to home, some anglers experiment with taking bream, sunfish, and other fish not even thought of as sport fish on flies and, even more exotic, fish like carp that don't even eat flies.

The study of aquatic entomology and development of more precise imitations of flies may become the focus for other anglers seeking to break new ground. For still others, the challenge is more internal. One form it takes is in improving casting and other fishing techniques so as to catch fish in new places or situations.

Another realm of experience lies beyond the quest for tangible, quantifiable proof of one's fishing prowess. It's the pleasure that comes from the simple act of angling. Angling becomes its own reward; nothing more is required. Almost certainly, one must go through the big fish, many fish stage to understand that a more profound satisfaction is possible. Our instinct is always to want more. When followed, it dooms us to perpetual frustration. There will always be more and bigger fish to catch, or some more distant goal to reach. At some point, many of us figure this out and jump off the reach-for-success ladder. But we must have had some success first to understand the process. For most of us, success is the release from the need for more success.

One may speculate whether in this ultimate stage of fly-fishing appreciation one actually needs to catch fish. The Chinese philosopher Chaing Tzu-Ya thought not; his view was that a line in the water without bait or hook was enough. My view is that this isn't angling; it's something else, perhaps contemplation with a line in the water. The same holds true for fishing in water where one knows there are no fish. Angling presupposes a desire to catch fish. To catch fish is better than not to catch fish, but the point is, not catching fish is not failure. Experienced, mature anglers derive pleasure from casting a fly over water they believe to hold fish although, if truth be told, seeing the fish rise enhances the pleasure. It sharpens the senses, gets the adrenaline flowing and the heartbeat rising.

Fly-fishing free of the need to catch fish frees us to be attentive to what's around us—light, air, wind, water, trees, flowers, weeds, insects, birds and animals interacting with each other, and in general, life. We see beauty better. We also see life more as a whole, in which our place is small and temporary. Knowing that our moment is fleeting, we appreciate it more. All this may lead to wondering how what we see and feel relates to a power from which the spirit of life and our own souls seems to derive.

Of course, these musings on the ephemeral and eternal may be invoked by other phenomena. Hallucinatory drugs may produce similar thoughts albeit in a muddled way. But fly-fishing has a way few other activities do of clearing the head and allowing us to see life as it is outside our temporal trials and concerns. What permits this is the rules of the contest of fly-fisherman versus fish; we permit ourselves a minimum of the technical advantage humans have used to overpower the natural world and each other. We enter the world of the fish, merging ourselves in their medium and meeting them on their own terms. Our weapons are wit, instinct, and physical skill. However, we lose more often than we win. How humbling! But this is as it should be. We are not the centers of the universe; there are powers greater than we that will outlast us. Occasional reminders of our place in the larger scheme of things are helpful. That understanding also allows us to feel more at harmony with life, and thus more at peace with ourselves and the world.

The altered, sharpened vision that can come suddenly or with time was expressed by an eighth-century Japanese courtier commanded to leave one imperial palace for another:

> Gazing now
> on the stream of Kiza
> that I gazed on in the past,
> I see how, more and more,
> it has become bright and clear.

Even if we don't find through fly-fishing the *satori*, or awakening, which is the ultimate quest of the Zen Buddhists, or the mystic's direct line to the God of the Old and New Testaments, we'll enjoy, at least on some good fishing days, the serenity and connection with the larger, natural world reflected in a seventeenth-century Zen poem:

> A trout leaps;
> Clouds are moving
> In the bed of the stream.

BIBLIOGRAPHY

Aelianus, Claudius. *On the Characteristics of Animals.* Translated by A. F. Scholfield. Cambridge: Harvard University Press, 1958.

Alighieri, Dante. *The Divine Comedy.* Translated by Lawrence Grant White. New York: Pantheon Books, 1948.

Ashley, Maurice. *Great Britain to 1688.* Ann Arbor: University of Michigan Press, 1961.

Bergman, Ray, *Trout.* New York: Alfred A. Knopf, 1970.

Braekman, Prof. Dr. W. L. *The Treatise on Angling in The Boke of St. Albans (1496), Background, Context and Text of "The treatyse of fysshynge wyth an Angle."* Brussels: Scripta, 1980.

Drucker, Philip. *Indians of the Northwest Coast.* Garden City, New York: Natural History Press, 1955.

Flick, Art. *Streamside Guide to Naturals and Their Imitations.* New York: Crown Publishers, 1972.

Hackle, Sparse Grey. "The Grave of Theodore Gordon" in *Random Casts.* New York: Theodore Gordon Flyfishers, 1989.

Hoover, Herbert. *Fishing for Fun, and To Wash Your Soul.* New York: Random House, 1963.

Jennings, Preston J. *A Book of Trout Flies.* Camden, South Carolina: The Premier Press, 1984.

Lambert, Darwin. *Herbert Hoover's Hideaway.* Luray, Virginia: Shenandoah Natural History Association, 1971.

Leiser, Eric. *The Book of Fly Patterns.* New York: Knopf, 1992.

Martialis, Marcus Valarius. *M. Valerii Martialis Epigrammation.* Leipzig: S. Hirzel, 1846.

McClane, A.J., *McClane's New Standard Fishing Encyclopedia and International Angling Guide.* New York, Chicago, San Francisco: Holt, Rinehard and Winston, 1965

McDonald, John M. *The Origins of Angling.* New York: Doubleday, 1963.

Plutarch. *The Lives of Noble Grecians and Romans, The Drysdale Translation.* Chicago, London, Toronto: Encyclopedia Britannica, 1952.

Raban, Jonathan. "The Last Call of the Wild" in *Esquire,* April 1995.

Radcliffe, William. *Fishing from the Earliest Times.* London: John Murray, 1921.

Ronalds, Alfred. *The Fly Fisherman's Entomology.* Secaucus, New Jersey: The Wellfleet Press, 1990.

Schullery, Paul. *American Fly Fishing: A History.* New York: Nick Lyons Books, 1978.

Schweibert, Ernest. *Trout.* New York: E. P. Dutton, 1978.

Shakespeare, William. *Antony and Cleopatra.* London: Oxford University Press, 1962.

The Complete Fly Fisherman: The Notes and Letters of Theodore Gordon. Edited by John M. McDonald. New York: Lyons & Burford, 1989.

The New Oxford Annotated Bible with Apocrypha, Revised Standard Version. New York: Oxford University Press, 1977.

The Ten Thousand Leaves, Volume One. Edited by Ian Levy Hideo. Princeton: Princeton University Press, 1981.

Thoreau, Henry David. *Walden.* Boston, New York: Houghton Mifflin, 1995.

Walton, Izaak and Cotton, Charles, *The Compleat Angler.* Mount Vernon, New York: The Peter Pauper Press, (undated).

Watts, Alan. *The Way of Zen.* New York: Vintage Books, 1989.

Zen Poems of China and Japan, the Crane's Bill. Translated by Lucien Stryk and Takashi Ikemoto with Taigan Takayama. Garden City, New York: Anchor Press/Doubleday, 1973.